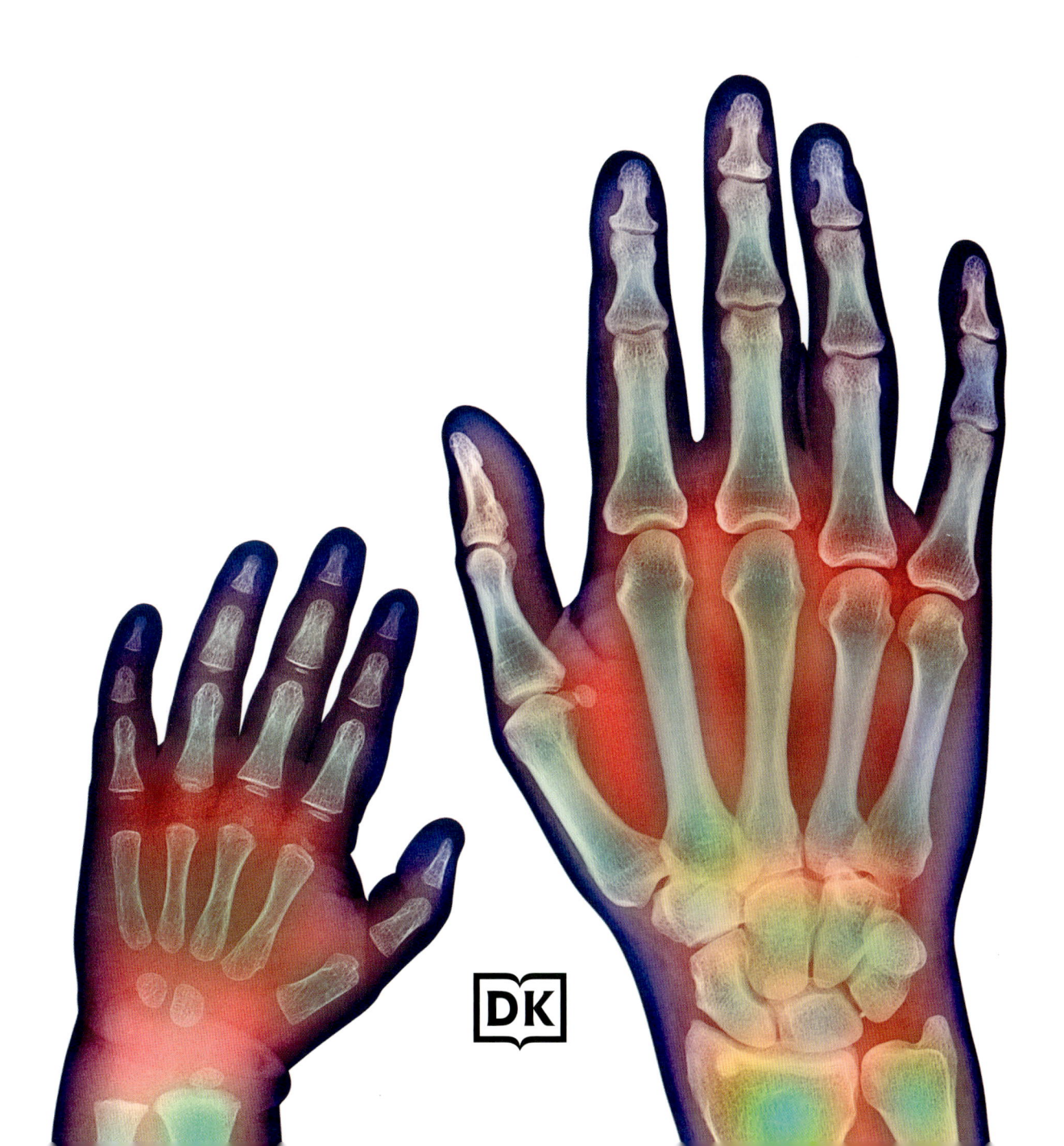

eyewonder
Human Body

DK

DK | Penguin Random House

THIRD EDITION
Senior Editor Rupa Rao
Senior Art Editor Ragini Rawat
US Senior Editor Shannon Beatty
Illustrator Aparajita Sen
Picture Researcher Ridhima Sikka
Deputy Manager, Picture Research Virien Chopra
Managing Editor Kingshuk Ghoshal
Managing Art Editors Govind Mittal, Elle Ward
Pre-production Image Editor Syed Md Farhan
Production Editor Vishal Bhatia
Production Controller John Casey
Senior Jacket Designer Nehal Verma
DK Delhi Creative Head Malavika Talukder
Associate Publisher Gemma Farr
Art Director Mabel Chan

Consultant Dr. Kristina Routh
Sensitivity Reader Dr. Kit Heyam

FIRST EDITION
Written and edited by Caroline Stamps
Designed by Helen Melville
Managing Editor Sue Leonard
Managing Art Editor Cathy Chesson
Category Publisher Mary Ling
Picture Researcher Marie Osborn
Consultant Daniel Carter

This American Edition 2025
First American Edition 2003
Published in the United States by DK Publishing,
a division of Penguin Random House LLC
1745 Broadway, 20th Floor, New York, NY 10019

Copyright © 2003, 2013, 2025 Dorling Kindersley Limited
25 26 27 28 29 10 9 8 7 6 5 4 3 2 1
001–348661–Aug/2025

All rights reserved.
Without limiting the rights under the copyright reserved above, no part of this publication may be reproduced, stored in or introduced into a retrieval system, or transmitted, in any form, or by any means (electronic, mechanical, photocopying, recording, or otherwise), without the prior written permission of the copyright owner.
No part of this publication may be used or reproduced in any manner for the training of artificial intelligence technologies or systems.

Published in Great Britain by Dorling Kindersley Limited

A catalog record for this book is available from the Library of Congress.
ISBN 978-0-5939-6753-9

DK books are available at special discounts when purchased in bulk for sales promotions, premiums, fund-raising, or educational use.
For details, contact: DK Publishing Special Markets,
1745 Broadway, 20th Floor, New York, NY 10019
SpecialSales@dk.com

Printed and bound in China

www.dk.com

MIX
Paper | Supporting responsible forestry
FSC® C018179

This book was made with Forest Stewardship Council™ certified paper—one small step in DK's commitment to a sustainable future.
Learn more at www.dk.com/uk/information/sustainability

Contents

4–5
Everyone looks different...

6–7
... but we are all alike inside

8–9
A growing baby

10–11
Super skin

12–13
A bag of bones

14–15
Hairy stuff

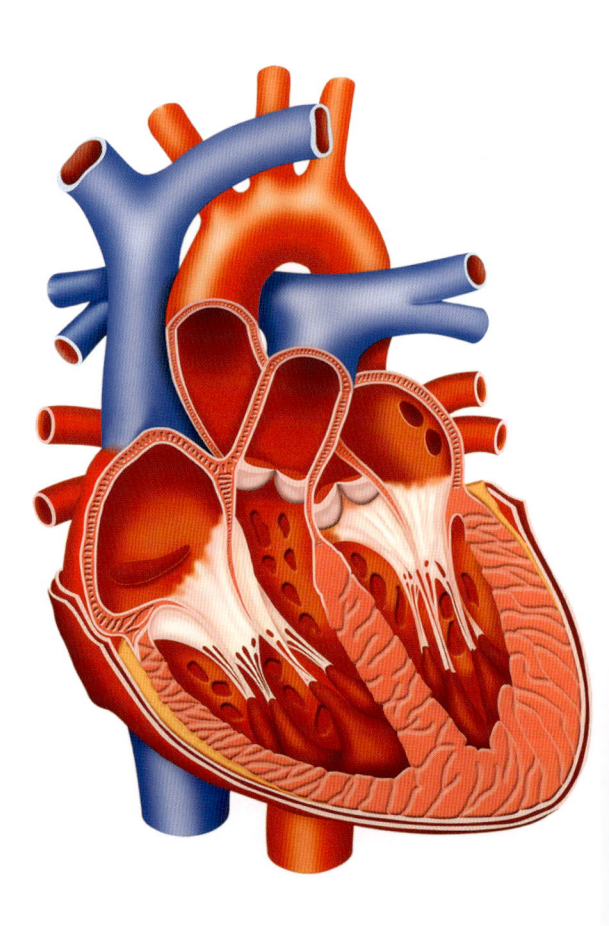

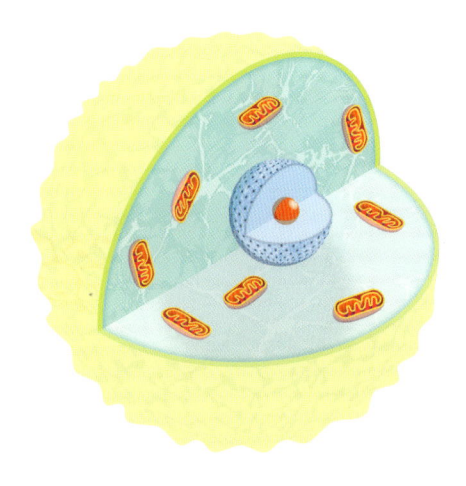

16–17
Move that body

18–19
Pump that blood!

20–21
Puff, puff

22–23
Germ invasion

24–25
Fighting back

26–27
Let's talk!

28–29
Brainbox

30–31
Touch

32–33
Listen up!

34–35
Eye spy

36–37
Smelly stuff

38–39
Fun with taste

40–41
Take a bite

42–43
Digesting food

44–45
Sleep tight

46–47
Facts match

48–49
Think away!

50–51
What's this?

52–53
Find the way!

54–55
Glossary

56
Index and Acknowledgments

Everyone looks different...

Tall, short, straight-haired, curly-haired... Even though most human beings have two eyes, a nose, two arms, and so on, we still look so different from each other that we can recognize people without confusion.

Human beings are different in all sorts of ways... but we are all made up of blood, bones, and organs.

Fast facts

The average human body contains enough iron to make a nail 1 in (2.5 cm) long.

People inherit certain features (such as hair color or body shape) from their biological parents.

Human hair is made of a substance called keratin, but its color is determined by the amount of another substance called melanin.

Twin tales

Identical twins look alike and that is because they develop at the same time, when one fertilized egg splits into two.

... but we are all alike inside

The human body contains many organs. Skin is an organ. It is wrapped around a framework of bones and other organs such as the heart, the brain, and the lungs.

Building blocks

A number of organs may make up each body system. For example, the stomach, liver, intestines, gallbladder, and pancreas make up your digestive system.

Your body is a collection of systems, each of which has a role to play.

Lung

Heart

Liver

Stomach

Large intestine

Small intestine

Many of your organs are packed neatly into your torso (the part without the head and limbs).

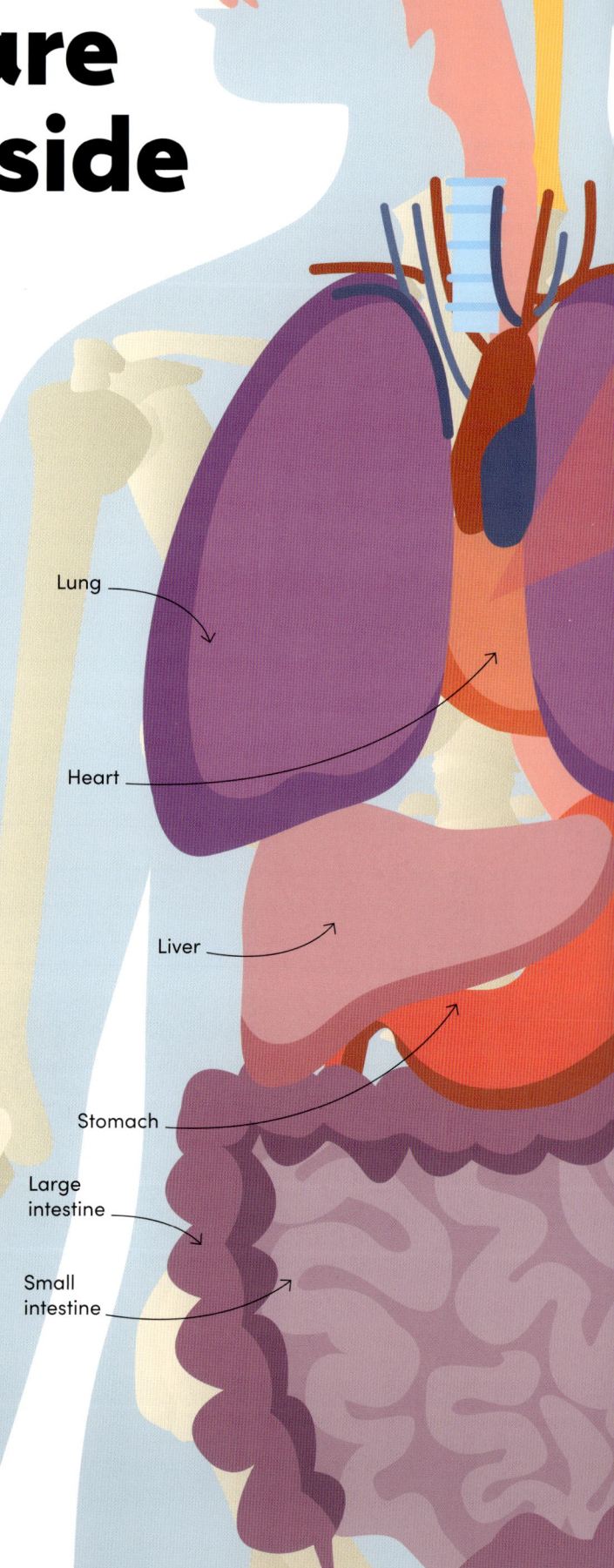

What does an organ do?
Organs work together to keep you alive, and each does a different job. The heart, which is part of the cardiovascular system, pumps blood to all parts of the body.

Made of tissue
Organs are made up of tissue, which is made of groups of similar cells. These magnified cells are from the heart.

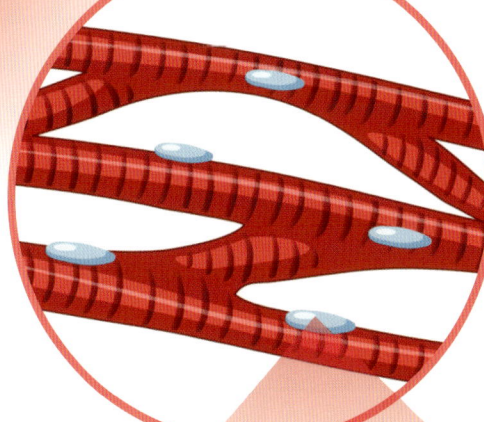

Lung

Your body has about 30 trillion cells.

Nucleus

Cell

Different cells
Cells are different depending on the organ they are a part of—skin cells, for example, are different than bone cells. Most cells have a nucleus—their control center.

A growing baby

A baby starts as a fertilized egg cell growing inside the womb. At first it is a mass of cells, which develops tissues and organs in time. Most babies spend about 40 weeks growing in the womb.

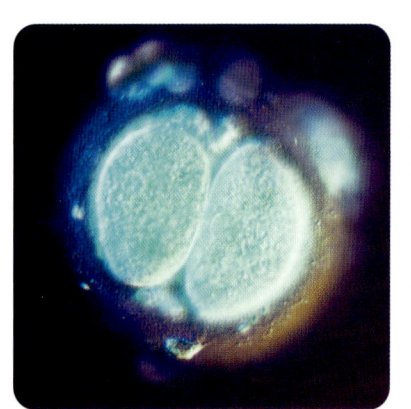

One cell at a time
When a fertilized egg begins to divide, it becomes a ball of cells. It is full of instructions for what the baby will look like.

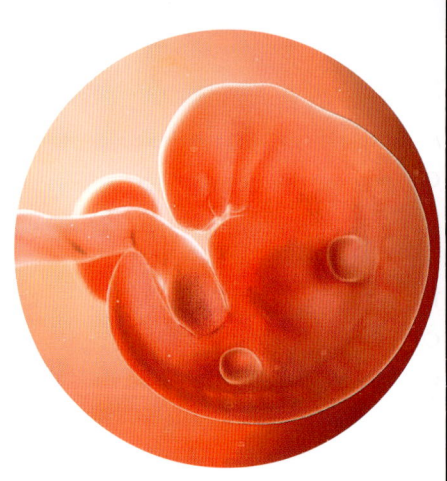

Legs here, arms there...
Between weeks 5 and 10, the growing baby changes from the size of an apple seed to the size of an olive. Its new limbs are beginning to move.

It can hear you!
A baby can hear outside noises from around the womb. By the time it is full term, its hearing is well developed, so it can even recognize familiar sounds, such as voices.

Support system

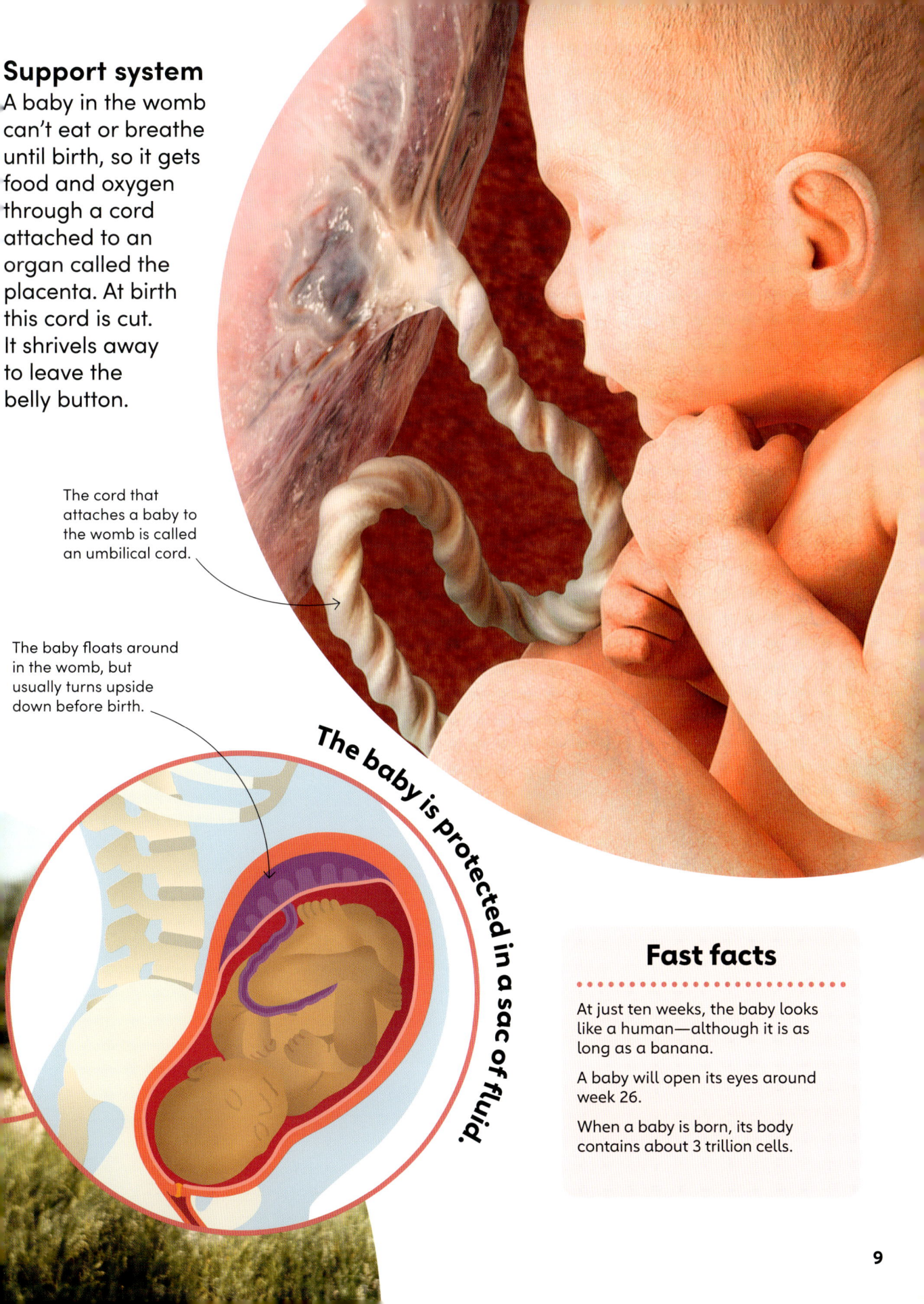

A baby in the womb can't eat or breathe until birth, so it gets food and oxygen through a cord attached to an organ called the placenta. At birth this cord is cut. It shrivels away to leave the belly button.

The cord that attaches a baby to the womb is called an umbilical cord.

The baby floats around in the womb, but usually turns upside down before birth.

The baby is protected in a sac of fluid.

Fast facts

At just ten weeks, the baby looks like a human—although it is as long as a banana.

A baby will open its eyes around week 26.

When a baby is born, its body contains about 3 trillion cells.

Super skin

Your skin is a fabulous covering for your body. It's stretchy and waterproof, and it protects you from germs.

In most places, your skin is about 1/16 in (2 mm) thick.

What's underneath?
Skin contains sweat glands, hair follicles, nerve endings, and tiny blood vessels called capillaries. Underneath, there's a layer of fat.

Cells lock together to provide a waterproof layer.

Flakes of dead skin

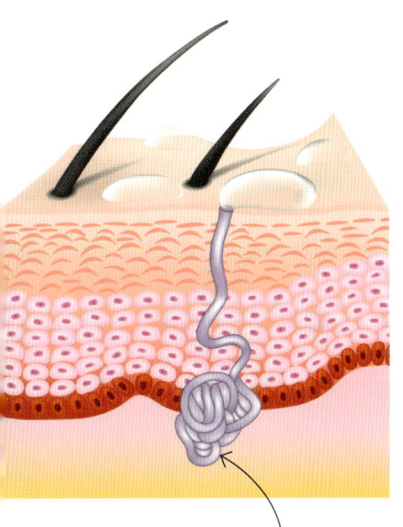

Sweat it out
You sweat to keep cool—but did you know that in a fingernail-sized patch of skin there are between 100 and 600 sweat glands?

Sweat glands sit in the deepest layer of the skin.

Heal that cut!
Cut yourself and a lot of activity in the surrounding skin causes the blood to clot. The resulting scab stops dirt and germs from getting in.

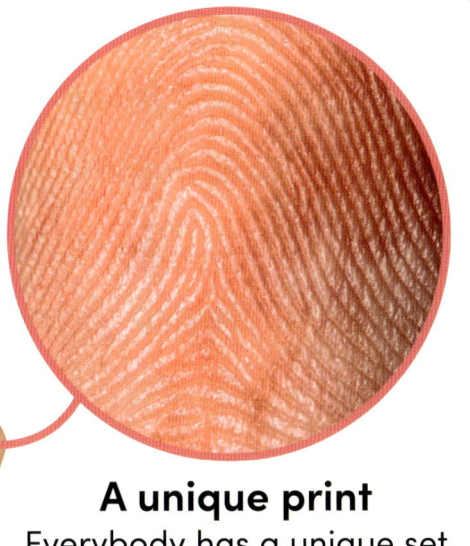

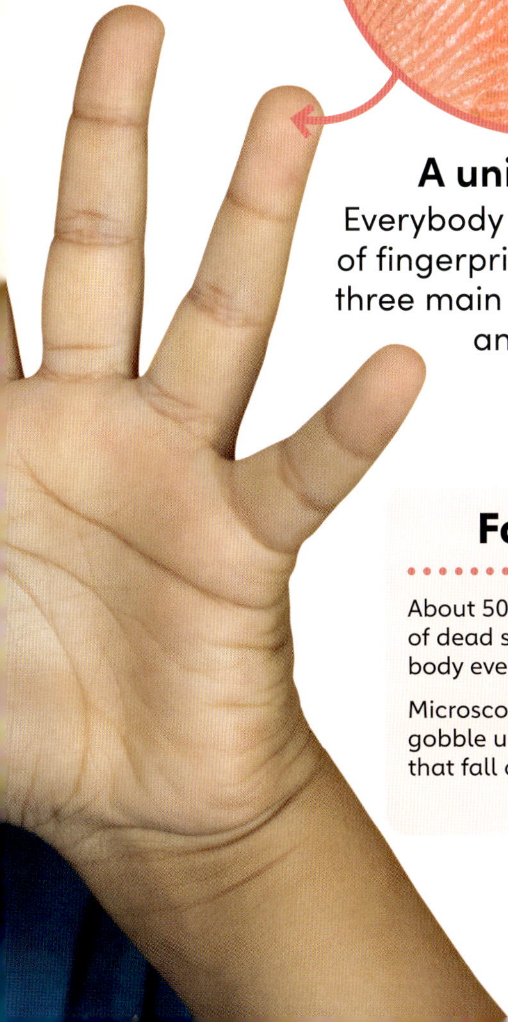

A unique print
Everybody has a unique set of fingerprints, but there are three main types: arch, loop, and whorl.

Fast facts

About 50,000 tiny flakes of dead skin drop off your body every minute!

Microscopic dust mites gobble up the skin flakes that fall off you.

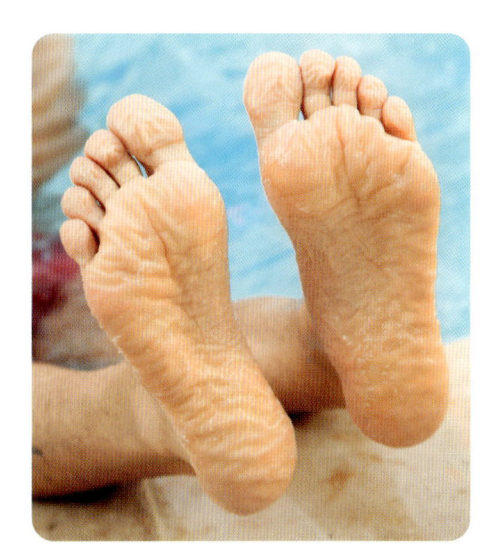

Wrinkly feet
Spend a long time swimming and your nerves tell the skin on your hands and feet to wrinkle up. This may help them to have a better grip.

A bag of bones

Bones protect your internal organs from damage and act as a frame to hold you up. They are linked together to make up your skeleton.

Fast facts

Compared to a steel bar of the same weight, a bone is stronger.

Most children have the same number of neck bones as a giraffe.

Bones need calcium from foods such as milk or leafy vegetables to make them hard.

The number of bones in the hands makes them very flexible.

Cartilage
A baby's skeleton is largely cartilage, the stuff that makes your nose flexible.

Bony hands
More than a quarter of your bones are in your hands. An adult has 27 bones in each hand.

The rib cage protects the lungs.

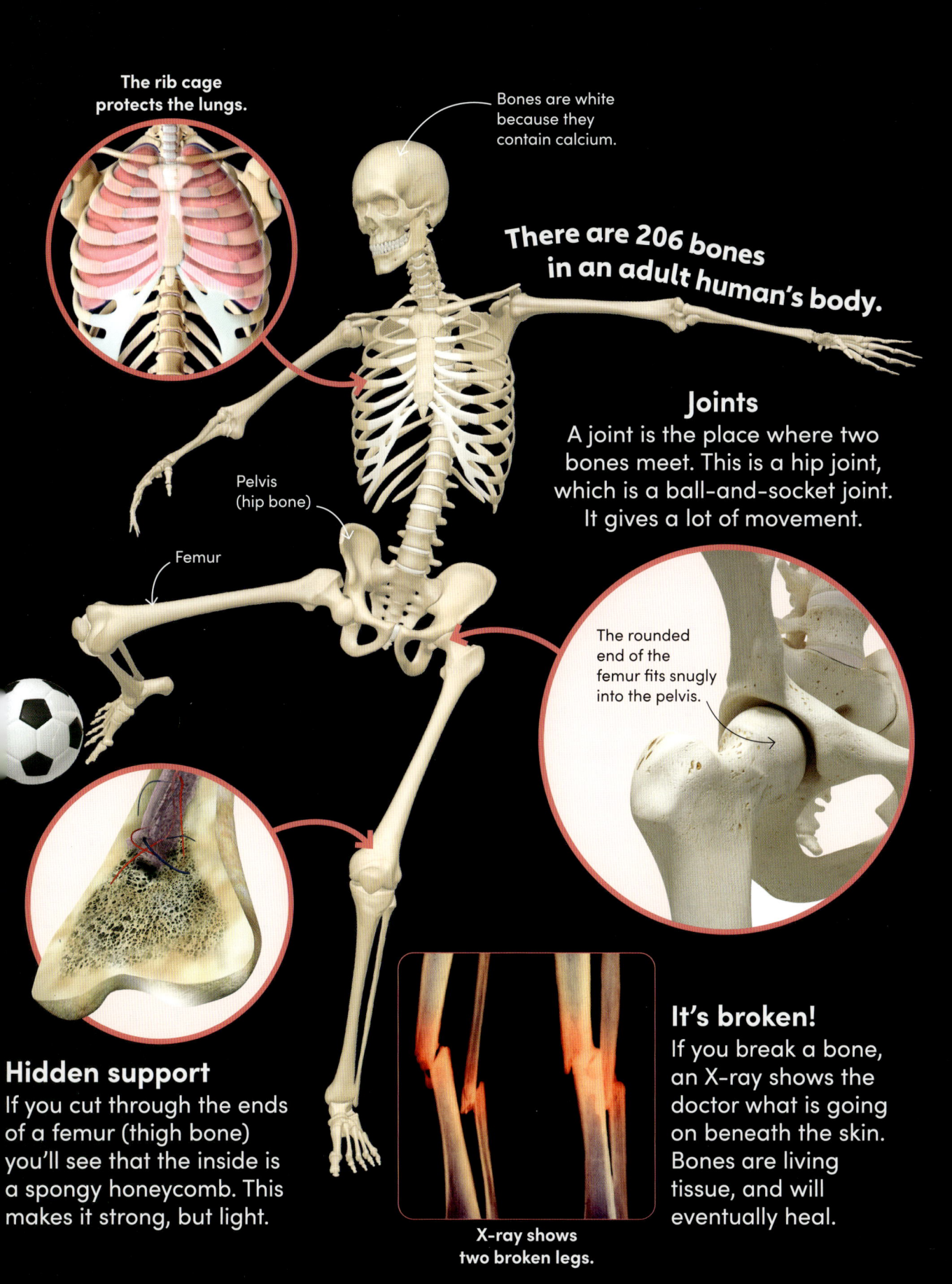

Bones are white because they contain calcium.

There are 206 bones in an adult human's body.

Pelvis (hip bone)

Femur

Joints
A joint is the place where two bones meet. This is a hip joint, which is a ball-and-socket joint. It gives a lot of movement.

The rounded end of the femur fits snugly into the pelvis.

Hidden support
If you cut through the ends of a femur (thigh bone) you'll see that the inside is a spongy honeycomb. This makes it strong, but light.

X-ray shows two broken legs.

It's broken!
If you break a bone, an X-ray shows the doctor what is going on beneath the skin. Bones are living tissue, and will eventually heal.

Hairy stuff

Your hair and nails are made of a substance called keratin—and most of it is dead. In fact, your hair and nails are only alive at the roots. That's why it doesn't hurt to cut your hair or trim your nails.

A hairy tale

Hair grows over most of your body, from follicles on the skin. The thickest is on your head where you have between 100,000 and 150,000 hairs!

STRAIGHT, WAVY, OR CURLY?

The shape of your hair—straight, wavy, or curly—is related to the shape of your hair follicles. Straight hair follicles are round, wavy hair follicles are oval, and curly hair follicles are elliptical (an elongated oval shape).

Straight   Wavy   Curly

Scratchy head?

If your head keeps itching, you may have head lice. You can see their eggs as tiny white spots in the hair above your ear.

A female head louse will lay 50–150 eggs during its lifespan of four weeks.

Head lice

Head lice love to cling to hair, suck our blood, and lay their eggs. To get rid of them, use hair conditioner on wet hair, and then comb it with a special fine-toothed comb.

Fingernails

Like hair, your nails are made of millions of overlapping plates of keratin. Fingernails grow four times faster than toenails.

About 20 percent of the people in the world have curly hair.

Each curly hair is spiral in shape.

Move that body

Humans have at least 600 muscles, and they are responsible for every movement you make, from blinking to breathing.

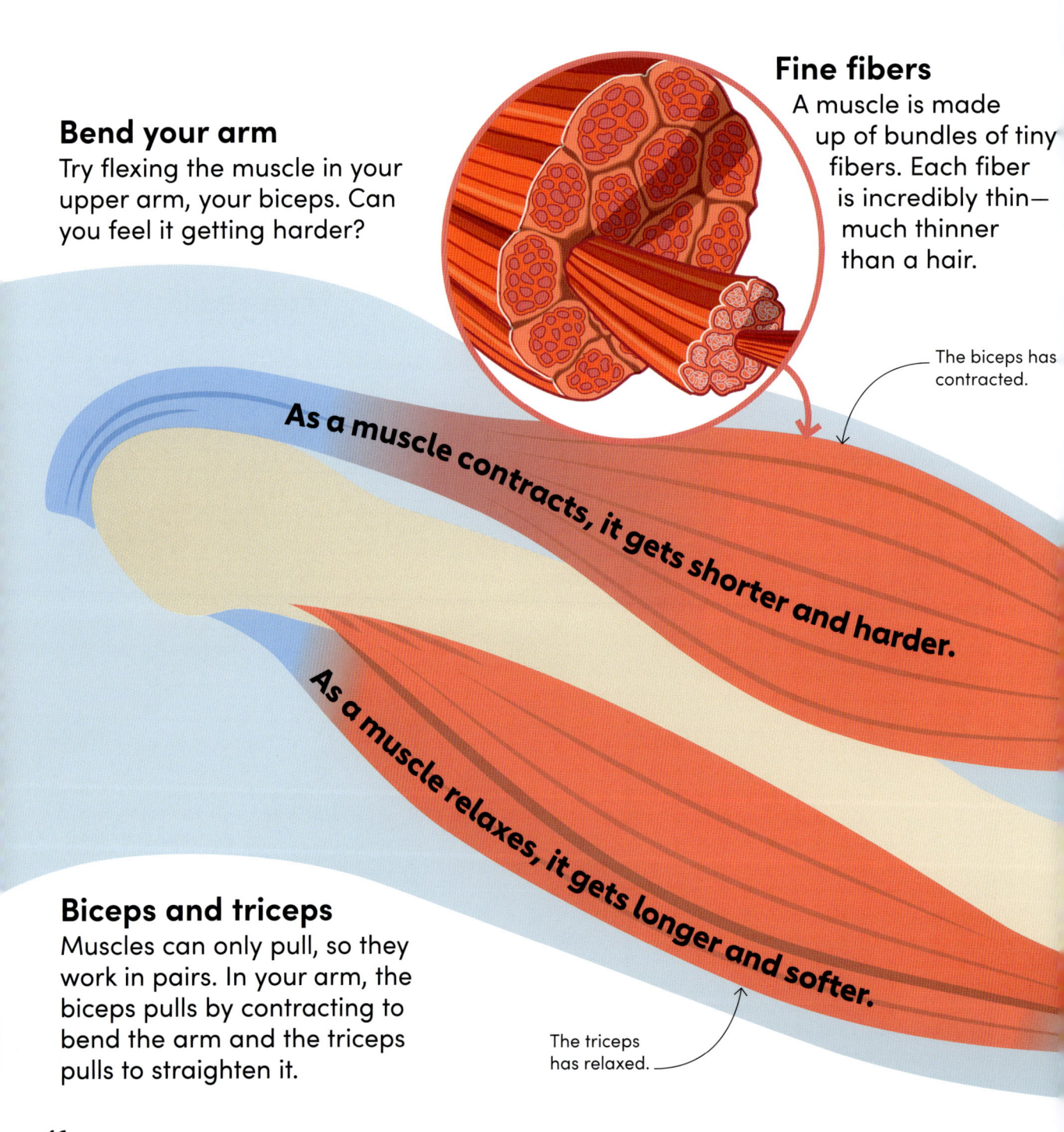

Bend your arm
Try flexing the muscle in your upper arm, your biceps. Can you feel it getting harder?

Fine fibers
A muscle is made up of bundles of tiny fibers. Each fiber is incredibly thin—much thinner than a hair.

The biceps has contracted.

As a muscle contracts, it gets shorter and harder.

As a muscle relaxes, it gets longer and softer.

The triceps has relaxed.

Biceps and triceps
Muscles can only pull, so they work in pairs. In your arm, the biceps pulls by contracting to bend the arm and the triceps pulls to straighten it.

16

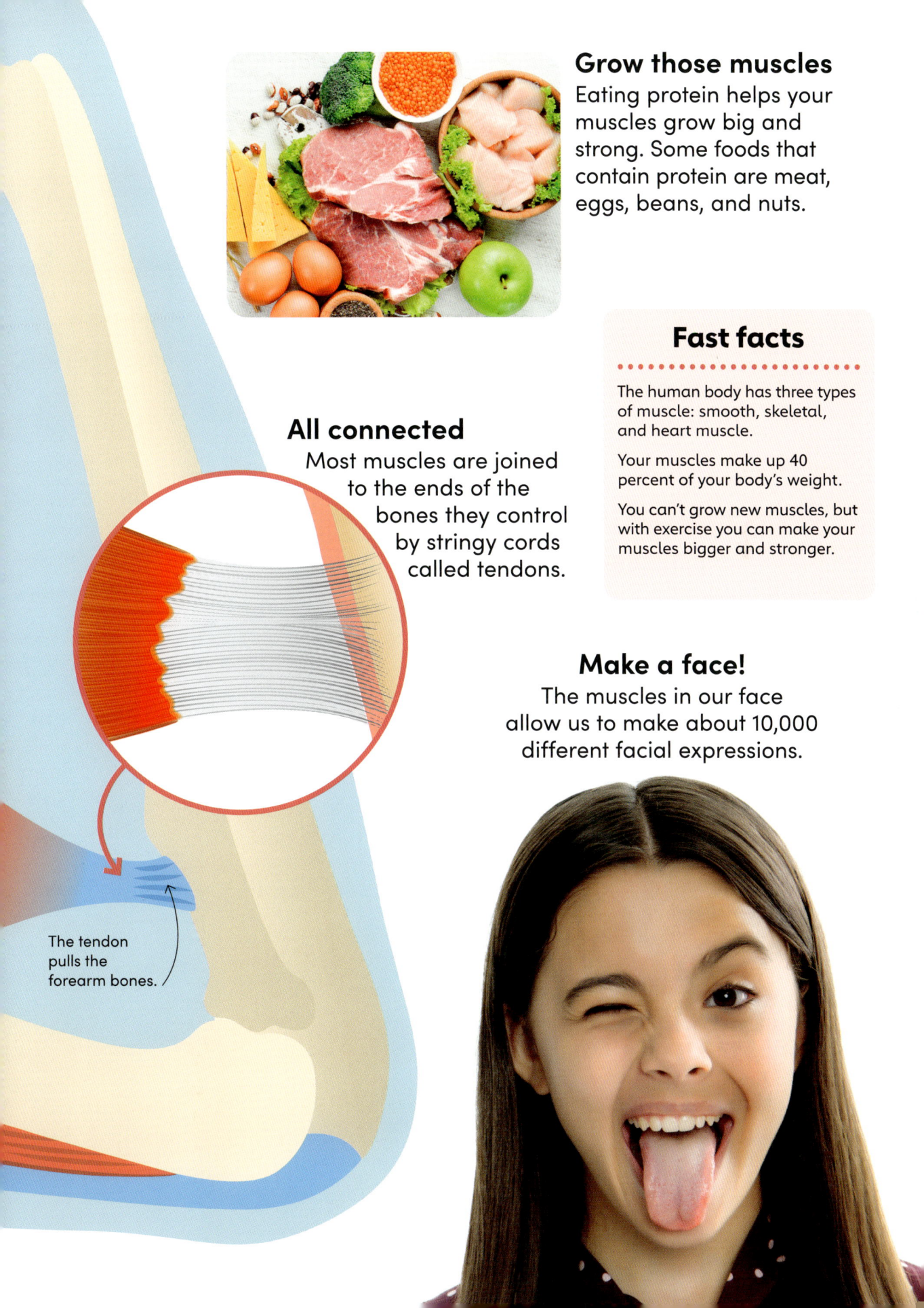

Grow those muscles
Eating protein helps your muscles grow big and strong. Some foods that contain protein are meat, eggs, beans, and nuts.

Fast facts

The human body has three types of muscle: smooth, skeletal, and heart muscle.

Your muscles make up 40 percent of your body's weight.

You can't grow new muscles, but with exercise you can make your muscles bigger and stronger.

All connected
Most muscles are joined to the ends of the bones they control by stringy cords called tendons.

The tendon pulls the forearm bones.

Make a face!
The muscles in our face allow us to make about 10,000 different facial expressions.

Pump that blood!

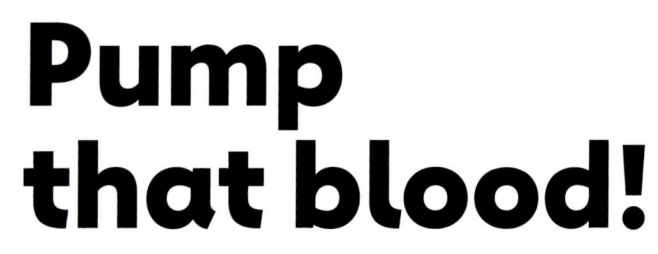

Can you feel your heart beat? This amazing organ never gets tired, even though it opens and closes about 100,000 times a day, every day, throughout your life.

Artery

Vein

A one-way system
Your heart beats to push blood around your body. Four valves ensure that the blood always goes the same way.

Tiny cords called heart strings stop valves from turning inside out when they close.

Blood system
The heart works together with a series of blood vessels in your body. These make up the cardiovascular system. Arteries take blood to other parts of the body, while veins brings blood back to the heart.

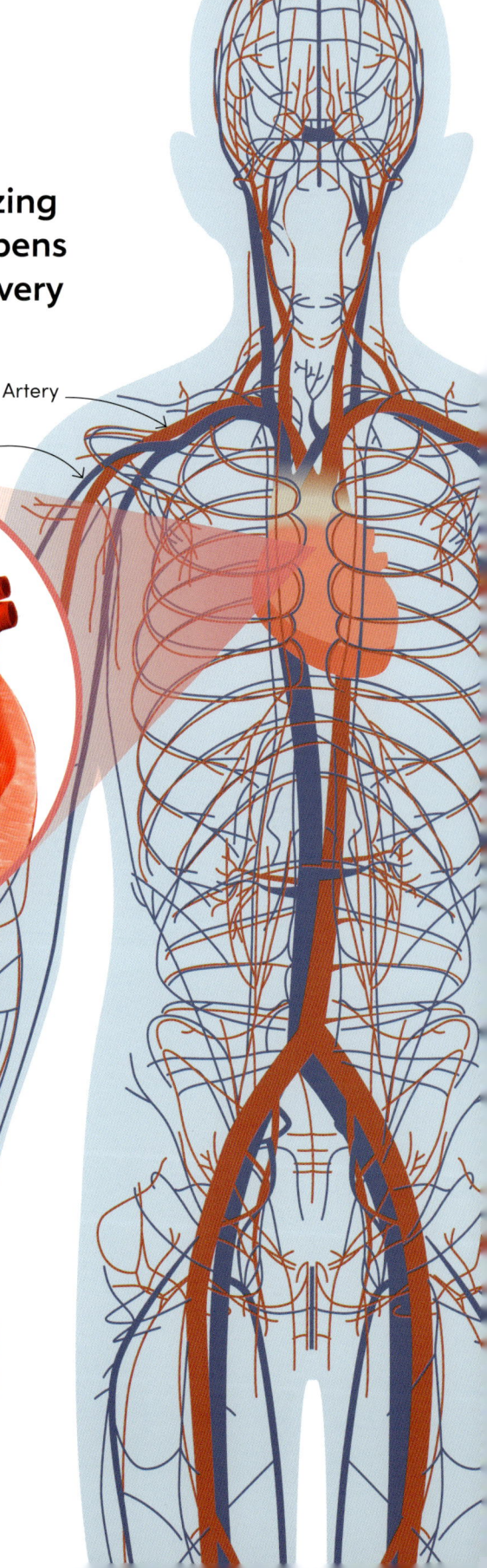

Plasma is a clear liquid.

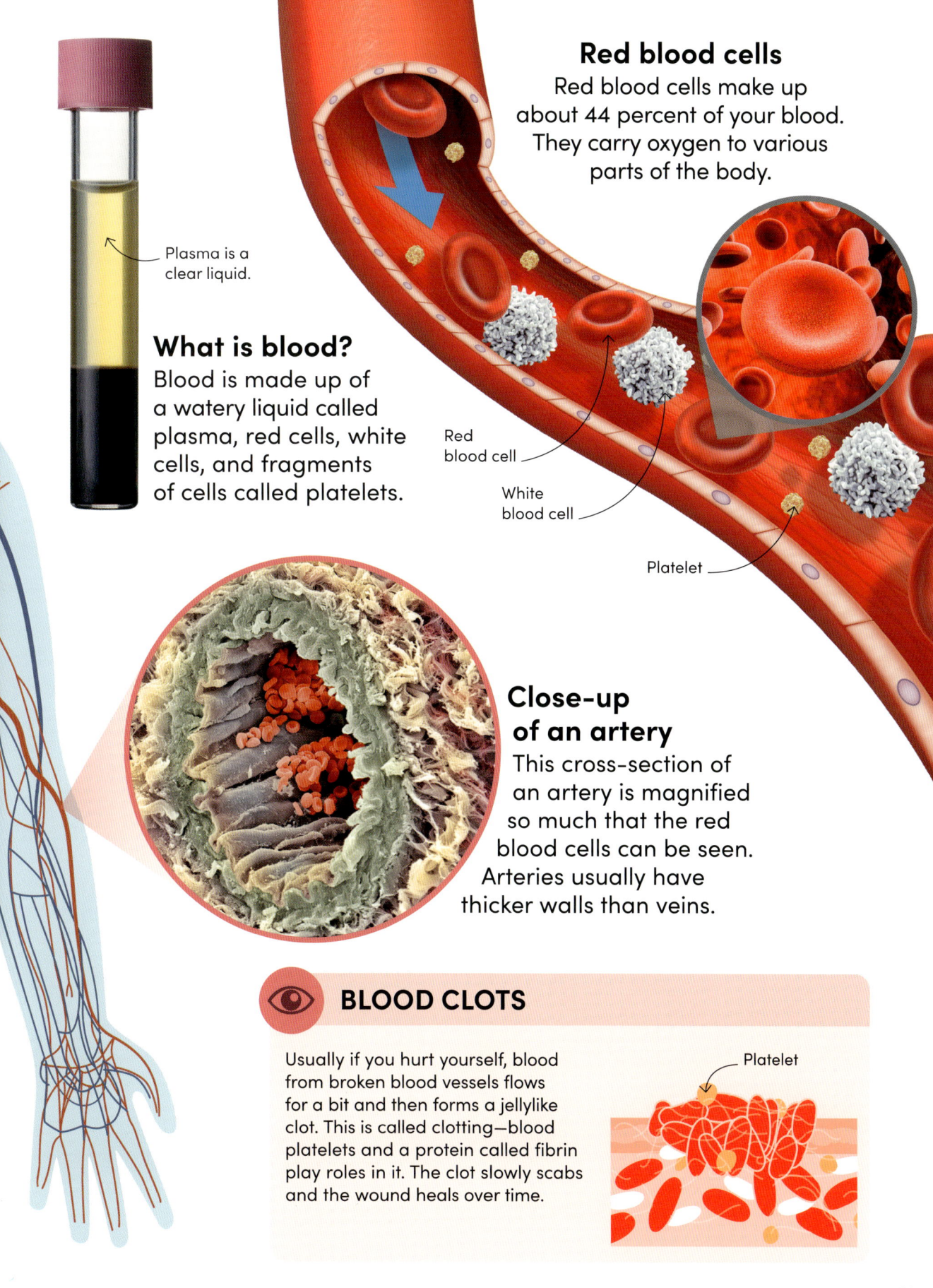

Red blood cells
Red blood cells make up about 44 percent of your blood. They carry oxygen to various parts of the body.

What is blood?
Blood is made up of a watery liquid called plasma, red cells, white cells, and fragments of cells called platelets.

Red blood cell

White blood cell

Platelet

Close-up of an artery
This cross-section of an artery is magnified so much that the red blood cells can be seen. Arteries usually have thicker walls than veins.

👁 BLOOD CLOTS

Usually if you hurt yourself, blood from broken blood vessels flows for a bit and then forms a jellylike clot. This is called clotting—blood platelets and a protein called fibrin play roles in it. The clot slowly scabs and the wound heals over time.

Platelet

19

Puff, puff

Believe it or not, you take about 23,000 breaths each day. With every breath, you take in oxygen, which you need to stay alive, and you breathe out a gas called carbon dioxide.

A wind tunnel
Air travels down your windpipe, or trachea, to get to your lungs. Rings of cartilage hold the trachea open.

Trachea

Rings of cartilage

Air tube

These spaces are air sacs called alveoli.

Taking oxygen
The air tubes get smaller and smaller until they end in millions of tiny air sacs called alveoli. Here, oxygen is taken into your blood.

Blowing bubbles

We can store oxygen for only a short time in our lungs. Also, unlike fish, we have no gills to remove oxygen from water. So we cannot stay underwater for long without an air supply.

Watery breath

Your breath contains water. If you breathe onto a cold surface, this water condenses into tiny droplets. That means it changes from a vapor into a liquid.

Fast facts

The lungs contain nearly 1,500 miles (2,400 km) of air tubes.

You breathe faster during and after exercise to draw more oxygen into your body.

Your left lung is smaller than your right lung to allow room for your heart.

👁 WHY DO I GET HICCUPS?

Hiccups happen when the muscle that helps to move air in and out of your lungs, your diaphragm, jerks uncontrollably. To stop them, you can breathe into a paper bag, sip very cold water, or hold your breath for a short time.

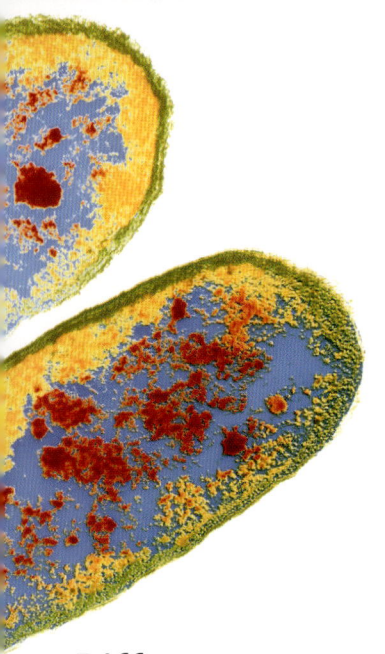

Germ invasion

Everywhere you go, you are surrounded by tiny living things called microbes. Many of these are harmless, but some can make you sick if they get inside your body. These are germs.

Different germs
Two types of germs are bacteria and viruses. Your body is good at keeping them out, but they are also good at finding ways in.

👁 WHAT CAUSES DISEASE?

Thousands of years ago, people believed that illness was a punishment from the gods. It was not until the 5th century BCE, some 2,400 years ago, that the Greek doctor Hippocrates told people that their surroundings, not magic, caused disease. He is known as "the father of medicine."

Vile viruses
Viruses are tiny—far smaller than bacteria. They cause many common diseases such as the common cold and the flu.

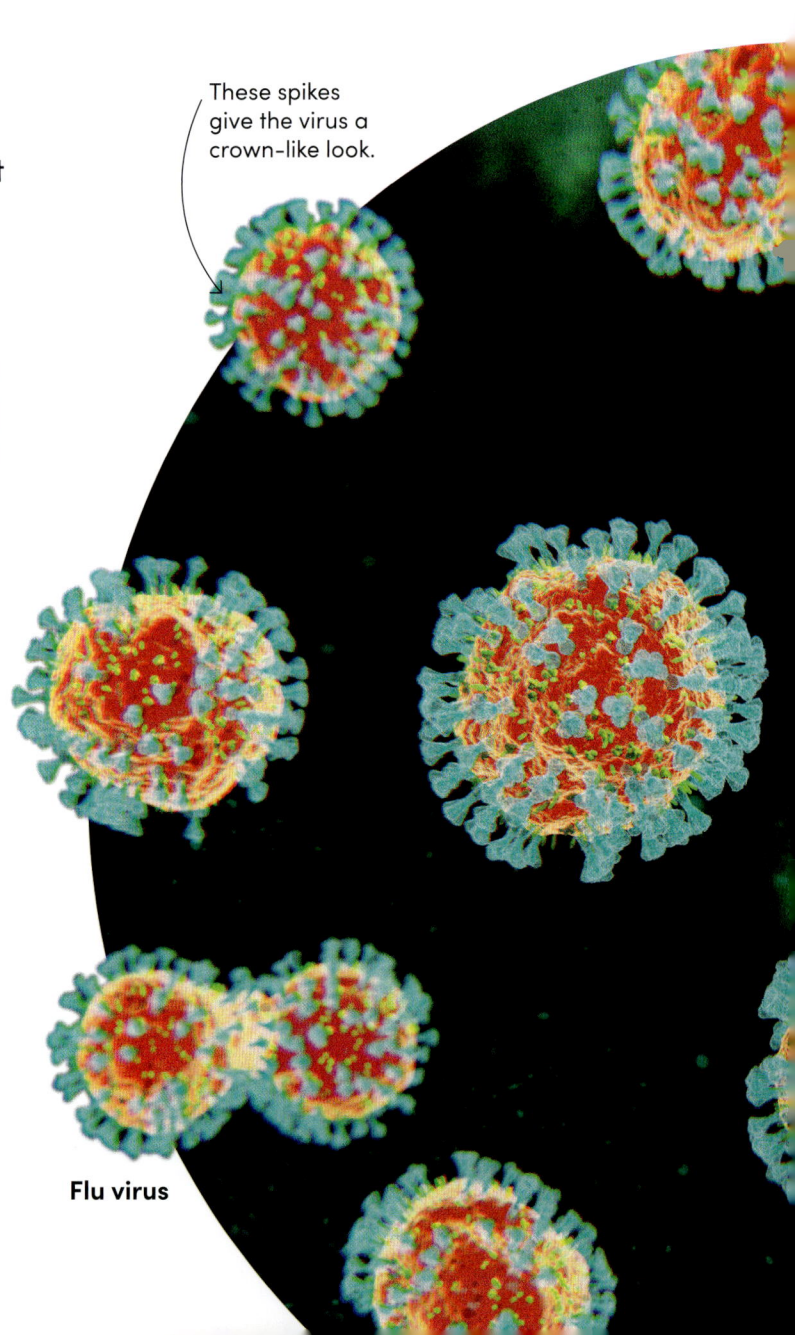

These spikes give the virus a crown-like look.

Flu virus

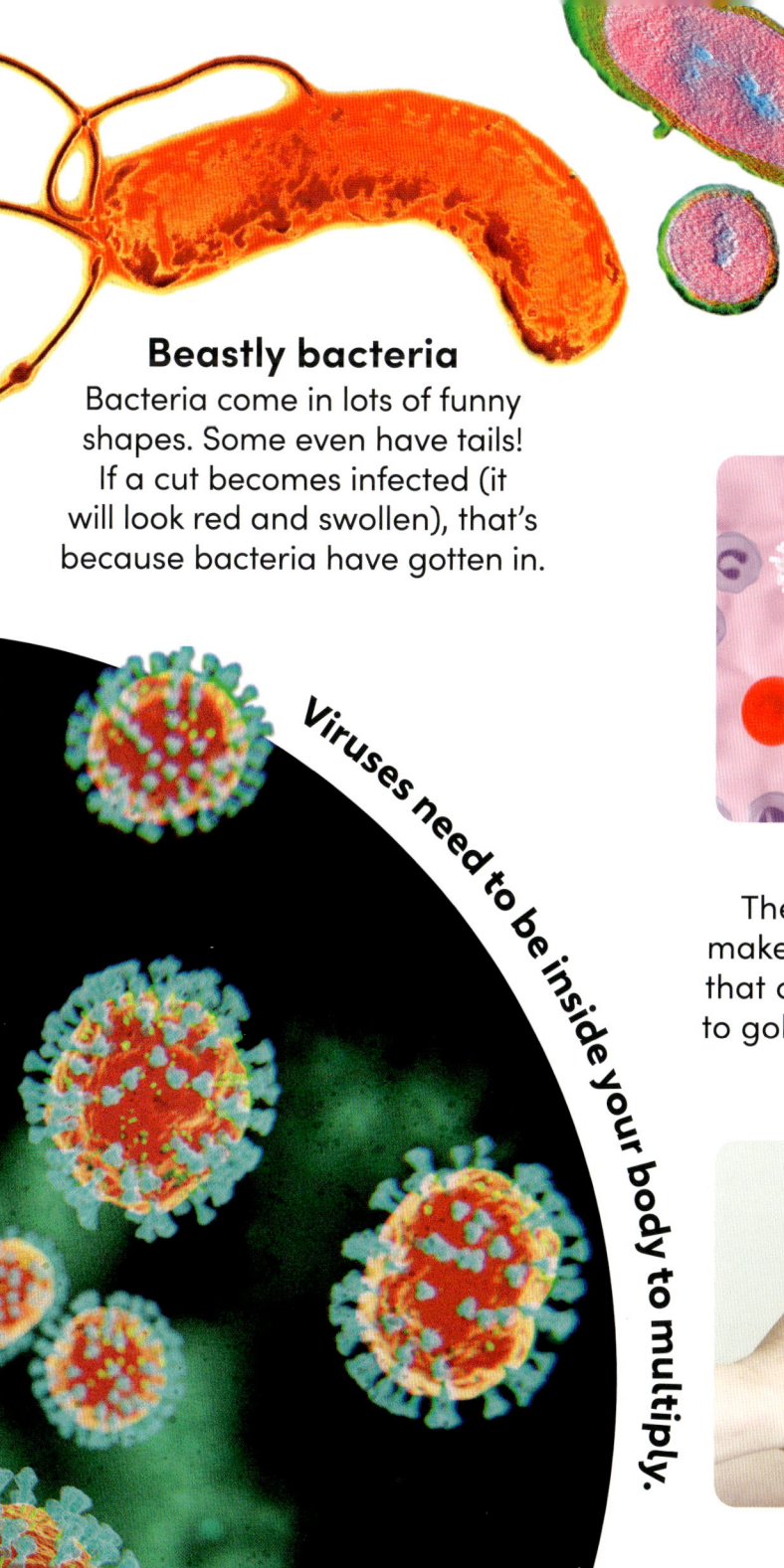

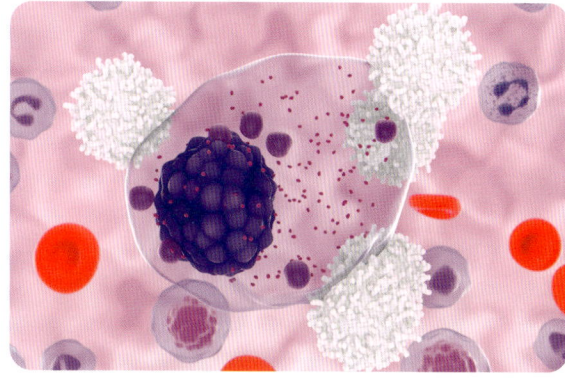

Beastly bacteria
Bacteria come in lots of funny shapes. Some even have tails! If a cut becomes infected (it will look red and swollen), that's because bacteria have gotten in.

This tiny bacteria's rodlike shape can be seen only under a microscope.

Viruses need to be inside your body to multiply.

Defend yourself
The good news is that your body makes things called white blood cells that can kill germs. They get together to gobble up a germ (as seen above).

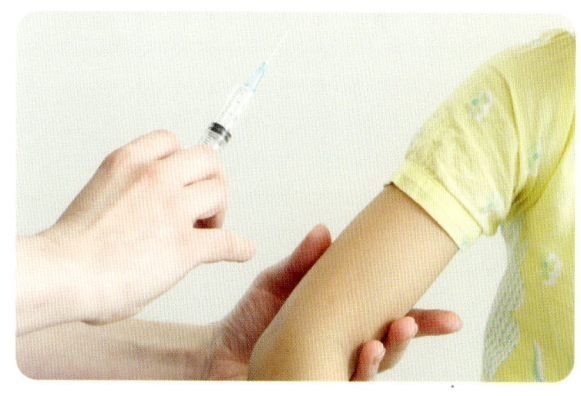

Help your body
Can you remember having injections called vaccines? These are special medicines that teach your body how to fight off infections and illness if germs get into your body.

23

Fighting back

Your body fights back to protect itself from any invasion by germs. In fact, white blood cells in your blood are fighters with one main job—to get rid of attacking germs.

Fast facts

Your body's defenses make up your immune system.

Your immune system remembers every germ it has ever defeated.

In many cases, if your body is attacked by a germ it has defeated previously, it knows how to fight that germ and protect you.

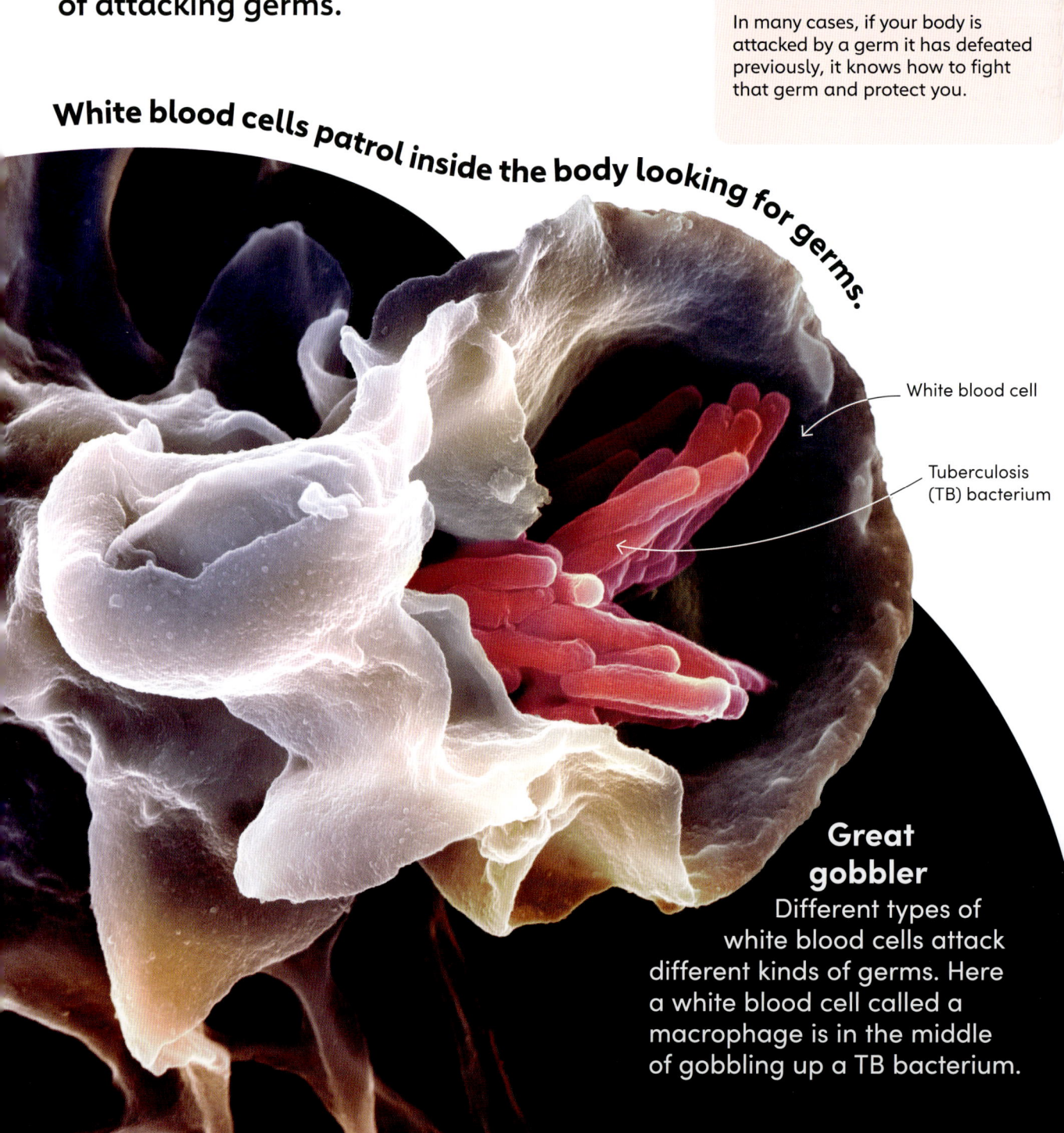

White blood cells patrol inside the body looking for germs.

White blood cell

Tuberculosis (TB) bacterium

Great gobbler
Different types of white blood cells attack different kinds of germs. Here a white blood cell called a macrophage is in the middle of gobbling up a TB bacterium.

The defenders

If a germ were to attack you, your body's first line of defense is the skin and the linings of the eyes, nose, and mouth—all of which carry chemicals that kill germs. If the germ gets to your stomach, chances are it will be destroyed by the stomach acid!

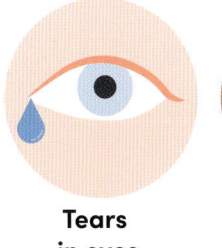

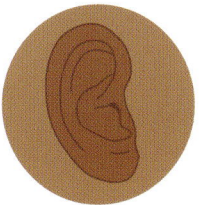

Tears in eyes

Wax in the ear canal

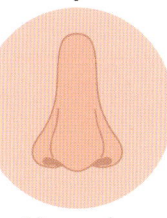

Mucus in nostrils

Saliva in the mouth

Antibody army

When your body recognizes a germ, it releases a weapon called an antibody. Trillions of antibodies attach themselves to the germ, flagging it as an enemy to white blood cells.

Antibodies stick to a germ.

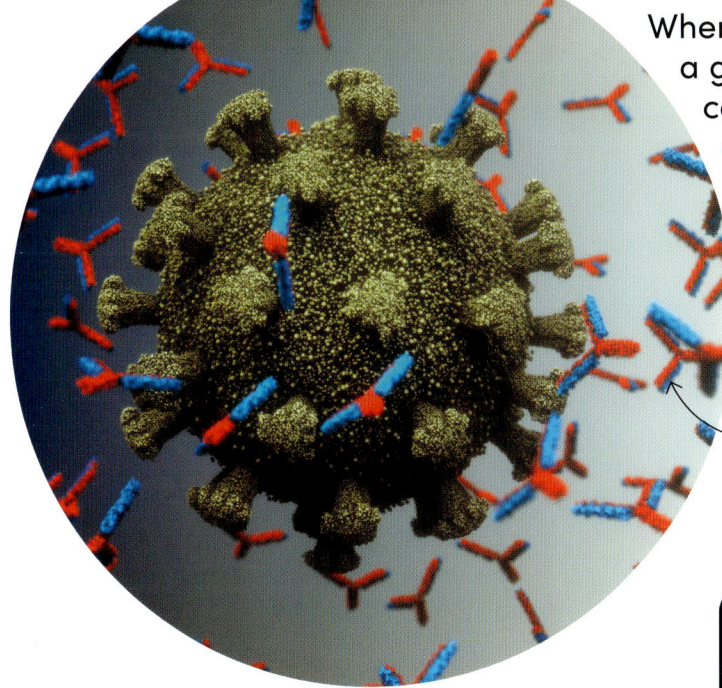

Allergies

Sometimes, we inhale or swallow dust, pollen, or other harmless substances. Our body wrongly thinks they are germs and the white blood cells attack, causing an allergy. It can cause itchy eyes, sneezing, or even troubled breathing.

Hide

Cuddle

Let's talk!

There are many ways of "talking," and not all of them are with your lips. The look on your face, the way you move your body, or the sign you make might tell people what you are thinking.

Whisper

Giggle

Baby talk
Babies can't talk, so they cry to let you know that they want something. From early on, they also communicate by eye contact and facial expression.

How do I feel?
Body language can say a lot about the way you feel. If you are excited, throw your arms in the air to let people know.

Making a word
You make sounds as you breathe out through your voice box, or larynx. Your tongue, lips, and teeth change the sounds into words. Some people may find it easiest to understand you when you speak.

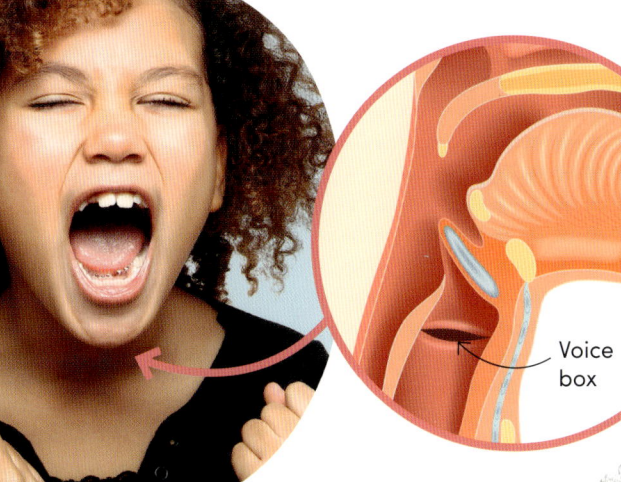

Voice box

Shout

American sign language (ASL) sign for "let's play"

Sign language
Signing is one way to communicate, sometimes used by some deaf people and some hearing people. They use their hands to sign words and to spell letters.

Brainbox

Step forward, touch something, talk, drink a glass of milk... everything you do is controlled by different parts of your brain.

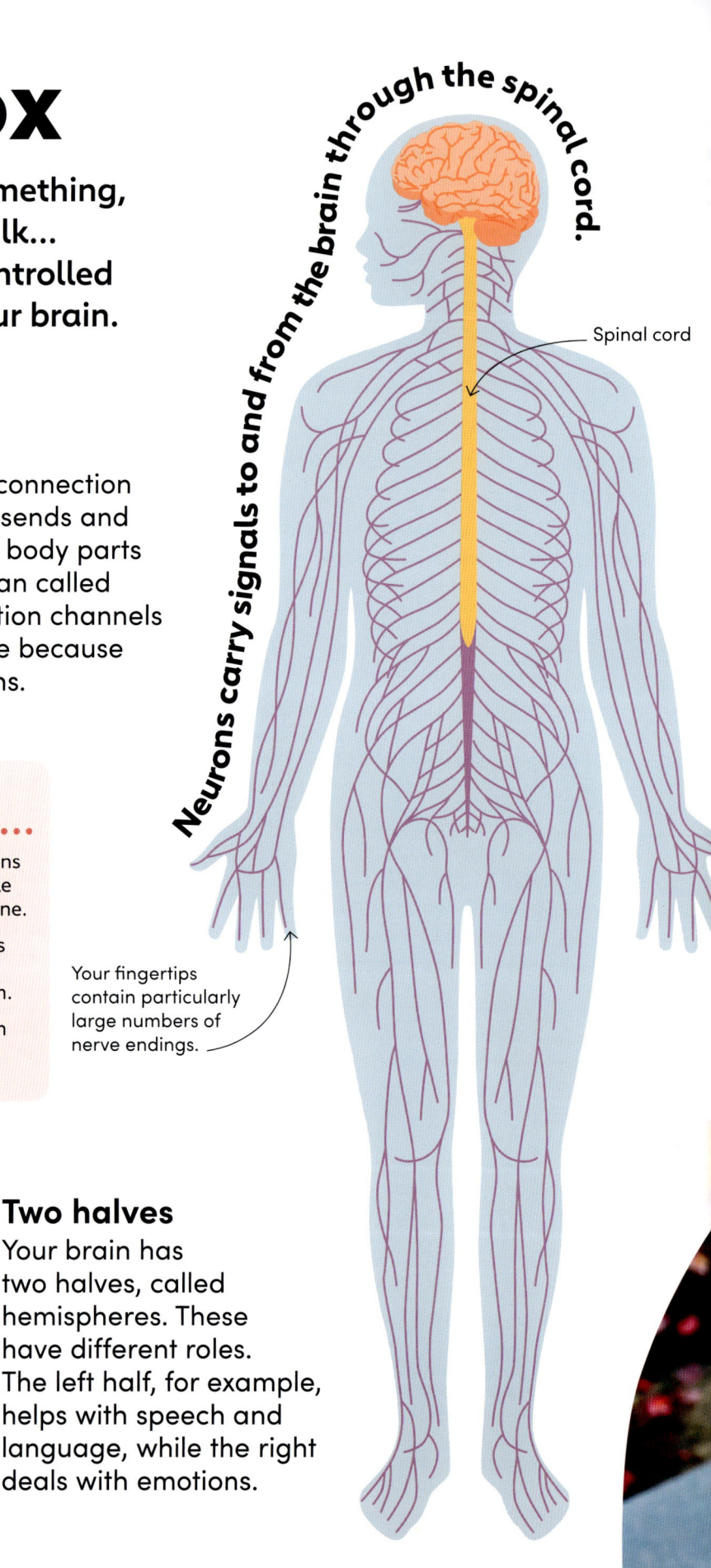

Brainy network

Do you have a fast internet connection inside your body? The brain sends and receives signals to and from body parts at high speeds using an organ called the spinal cord and information channels called nerves. This is possible because of special cells called neurons.

Fast facts

Nerves are made of bundles of neurons and tissue. The spinal cord is a bundle of nerves that runs inside the backbone.

The brain, spinal cord, and the nerves that go from the spinal cord to the whole body form your nervous system.

There are different types of neurons in the body.

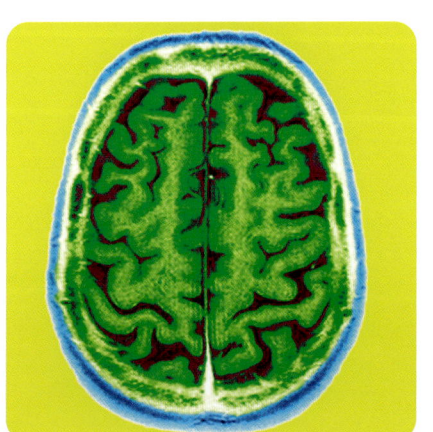

Neurons carry signals to and from the brain through the spinal cord.

Spinal cord

Your fingertips contain particularly large numbers of nerve endings.

Two halves

Your brain has two halves, called hemispheres. These have different roles. The left half, for example, helps with speech and language, while the right deals with emotions.

28

The top of a human skull is domed to make room for the brain.

The brain
As the brain grows, it wrinkles up to fit your skull, which acts like a protective crash helmet.

Neurons pass on the brain's instructions to the muscles.

Sight

Smell

Taste

Use those senses!
Licking an ice-cream cone requires a lot of brain power. Your eyes and fingers send messages about what you see and touch, while your nose and tongue help you to smell and taste the contents.

Touch

When you touch something, tiny sense receptors in your skin send a message to your brain.

Soft

Slimy

Smooth

Wet and cold

Many neurons

Your brain is the control center of your body. One type of neuron called sensory neurons bring it information from sense receptors. The brain then sends instructions to the different parts using motor neurons.

2. Your brain instructs motor neurons in the arm to tell the muscles to move to stroke the fur.

1. When you touch a soft and furry pet, sensory neurons send this information to your brain.

3. Motor neurons give your brain's instructions to the muscles, which move your arm.

Nerves are bundles of linked neurons.

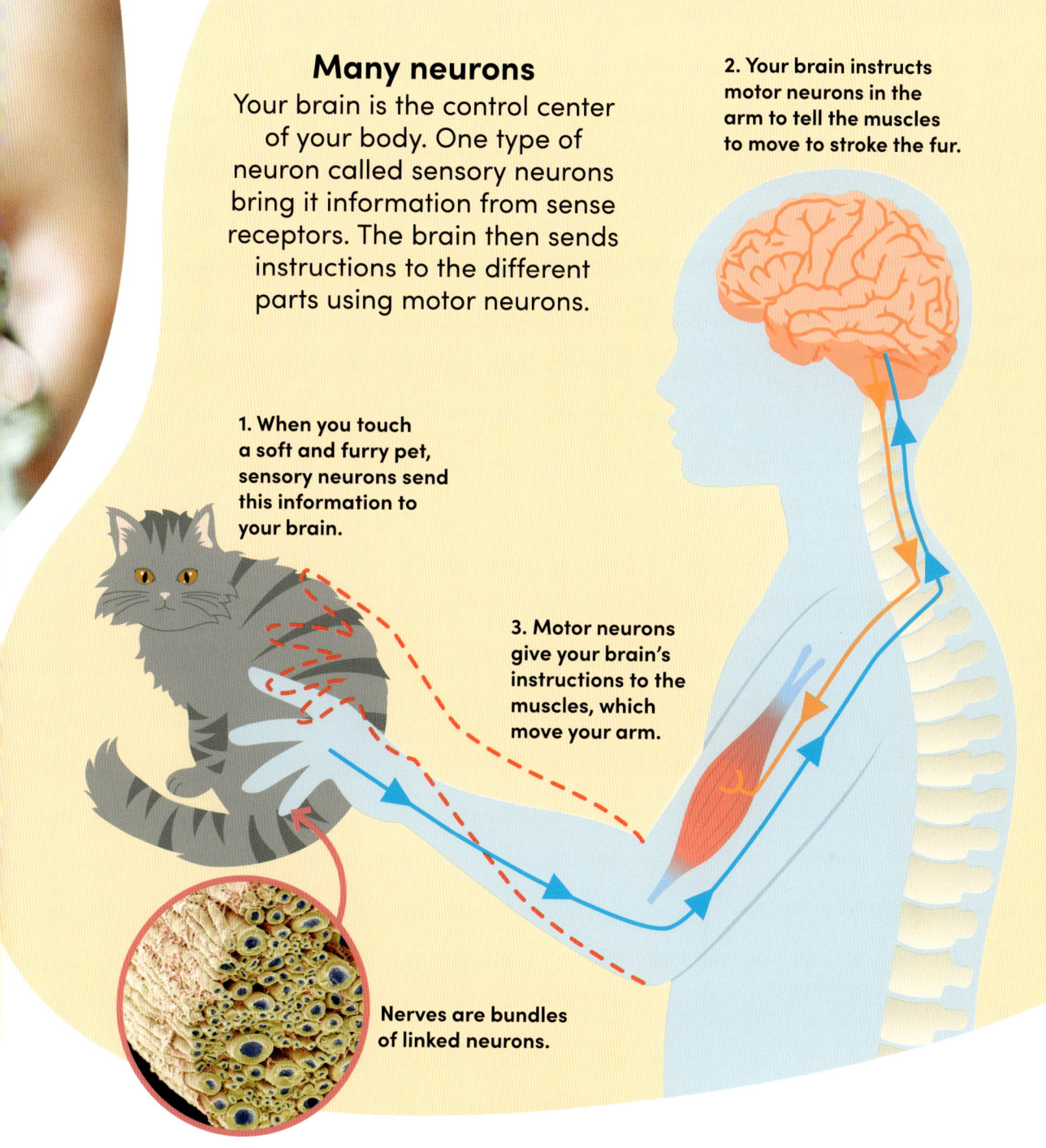

Fast facts

Sensory neurons sense pain, vibrations, and temperature.

You have about 3 million pain sensors, mostly in the skin.

Your body produces natural painkillers, called endorphins.

Diving reflex!

Under water, a baby that is one year old or younger will close a muscle to stop water entering its lungs. This is a reflex action, meaning the muscles react automatically.

Listen up!

Ears allow most people to hear. An ear has three parts: the visible outer ear, the middle ear (which has tiny bones), and the inner ear (which contains a coiled tube of liquid).

A waxy tunnel
The small pieces of dust and dirt that get into your ears are caught in your sticky ear wax.

Outer ear passes along incoming sounds as vibrations

There are 4,000 wax glands in each ear.

Fast facts

Human beings can tell the difference between more than 1,500 different tones of sound.

The stapes is the smallest bone in your body. It is shorter than a grain of rice.

Mammals such as bats and porpoises can hear high-pitched sounds beyond the range of human hearing.

People's ears get bigger as they grow older. This may be due to the effects of age in the ear tissues over time.

Hearing help
If someone cannot hear much, they are known as "deaf." Some deaf people wear hearing aids to make sounds louder and clearer.

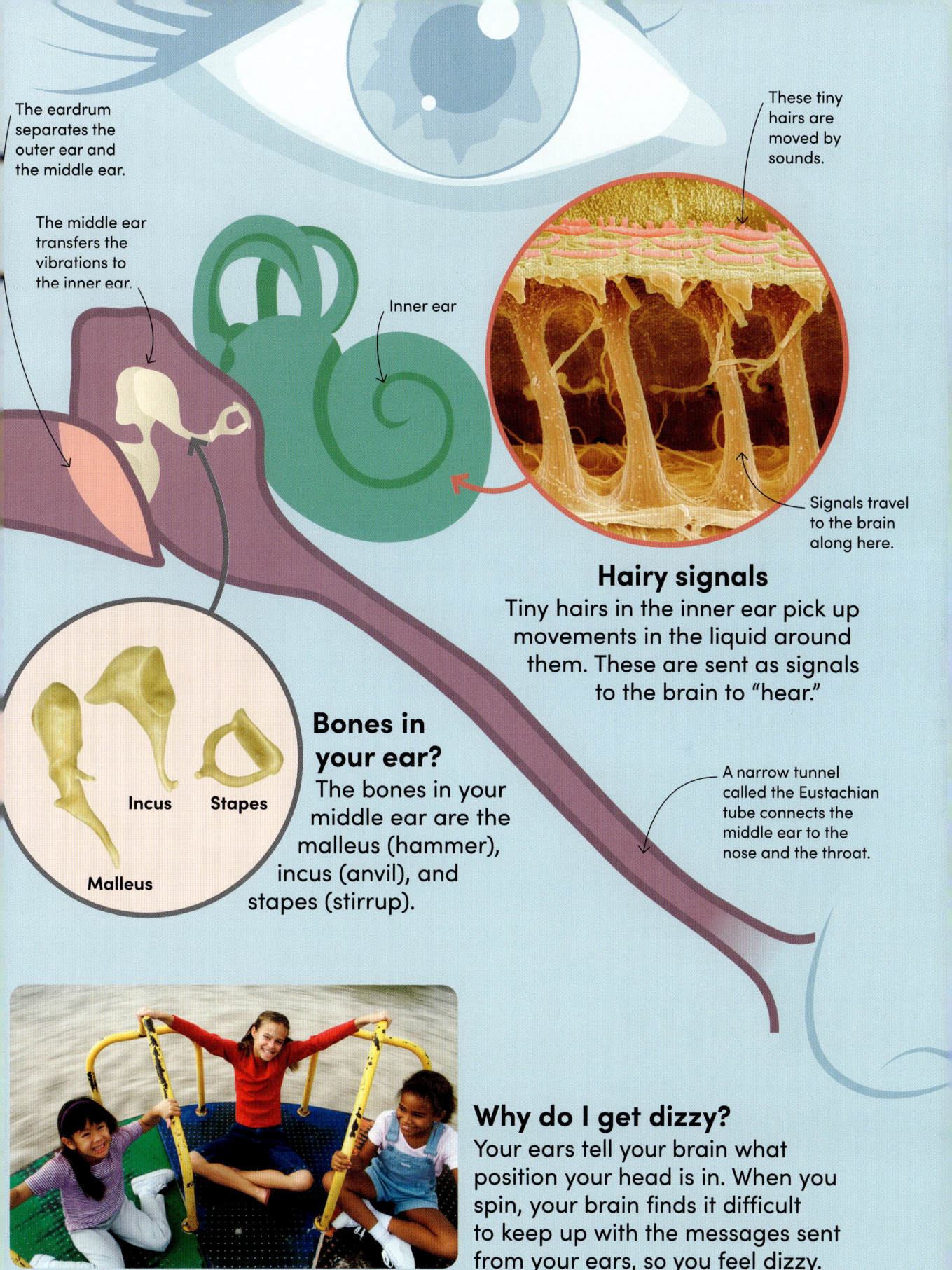

The eardrum separates the outer ear and the middle ear.

The middle ear transfers the vibrations to the inner ear.

Inner ear

These tiny hairs are moved by sounds.

Signals travel to the brain along here.

Hairy signals
Tiny hairs in the inner ear pick up movements in the liquid around them. These are sent as signals to the brain to "hear."

Incus Stapes

Malleus

Bones in your ear?
The bones in your middle ear are the malleus (hammer), incus (anvil), and stapes (stirrup).

A narrow tunnel called the Eustachian tube connects the middle ear to the nose and the throat.

Why do I get dizzy?
Your ears tell your brain what position your head is in. When you spin, your brain finds it difficult to keep up with the messages sent from your ears, so you feel dizzy.

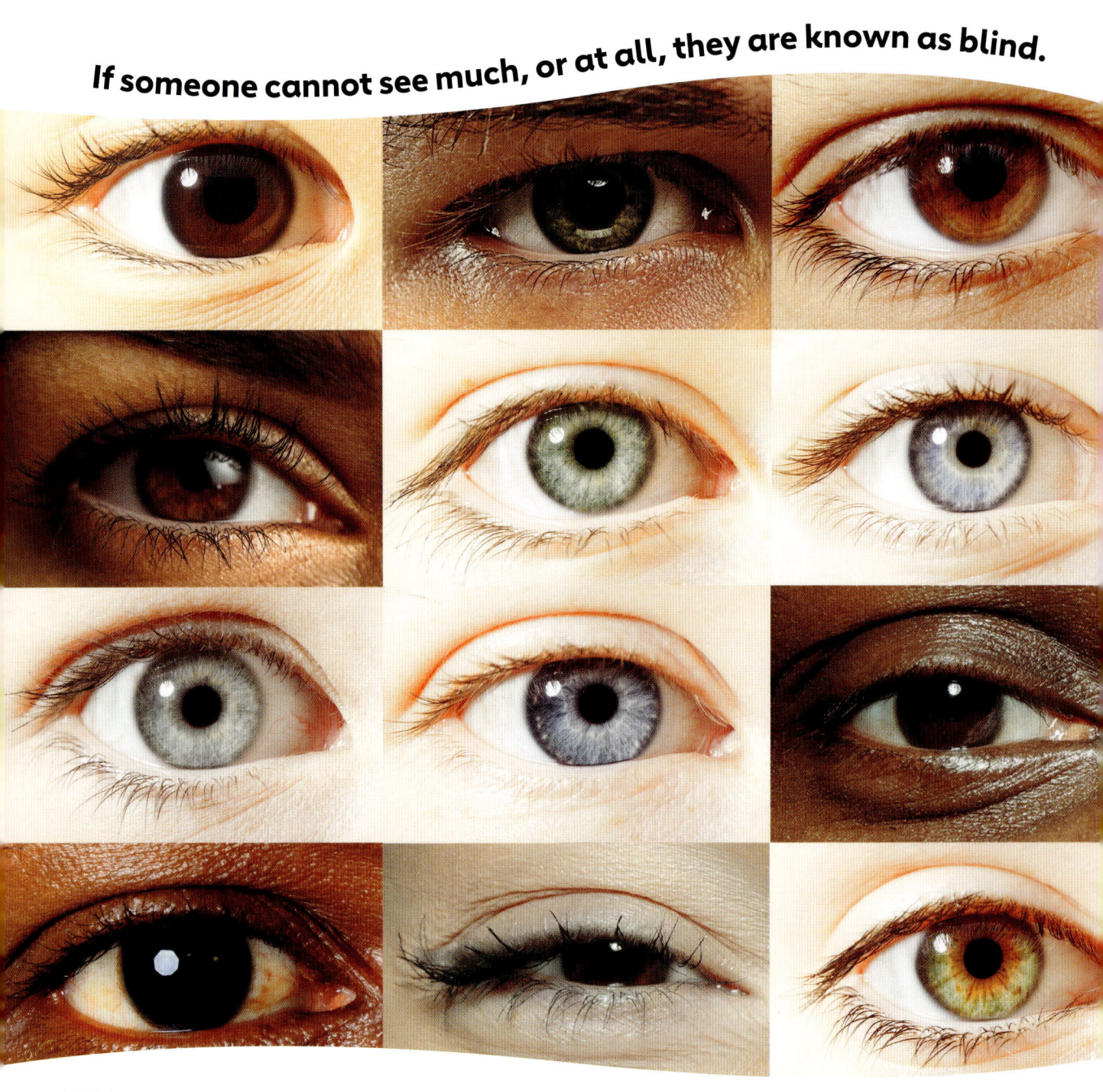

If someone cannot see much, or at all, they are known as *blind*.

Eye spy

Eyes allow most people to see. These soft, squishy balls in our head are well protected. They nestle in bony eye sockets and can hide behind the eyelids.

Vibrant colors
Blue, green, gray, or brown... what color are your eyes? The colored part of the eye—called the iris—can be a variety of colors depending on the amount of a substance called melanin.

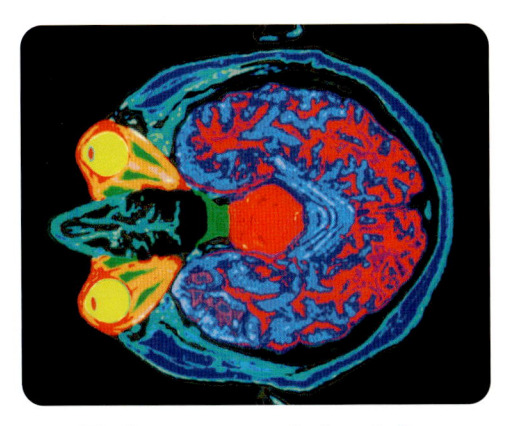

Take a peek inside
This picture shows the two eyes (yellow) in their eye sockets—separated by the nose. They connect directly to the brain.

A liquid camera
Your eyes are a bit like tiny video cameras, but filled with fluid. Light enters the eye through a hole in the iris, the pupil, and travels to the retina. Messages are sent to the brain, which tells you what you see.

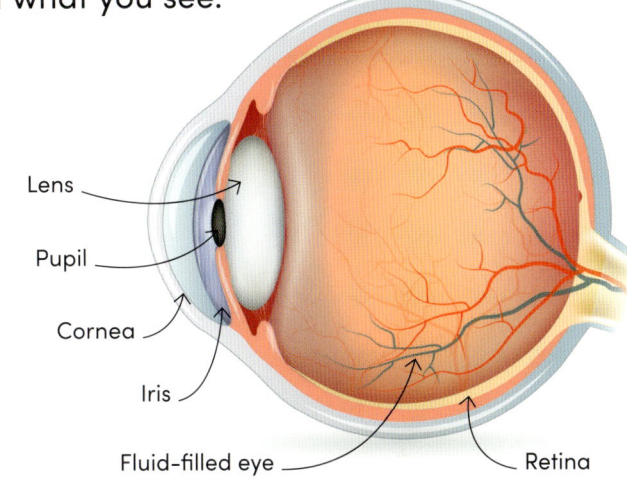

Lens
Pupil
Cornea
Iris
Fluid-filled eye
Retina

How big are your pupils?
Pupil size changes depending on the light—and what's around you. If you are looking at something you like, or you are thinking hard, your pupils may get bigger.

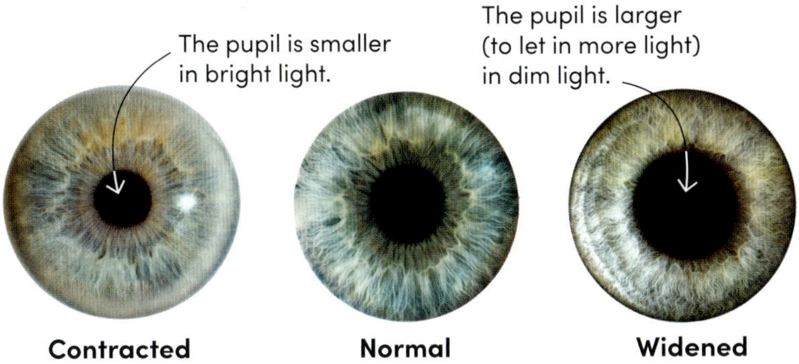

The pupil is smaller in bright light.

The pupil is larger (to let in more light) in dim light.

Contracted **Normal** **Widened**

Fast facts
You blink about 9,400 times a day.

Six muscles move each eye. They are kept busy, moving about 100,000 times a day!

If your eyes are each a different color, you have heterochromia.

What is color blindness?
The retina in the eyes contains pigments that detect color. If these are not working, you will have difficulty telling some colors apart. This is known as color blindness.

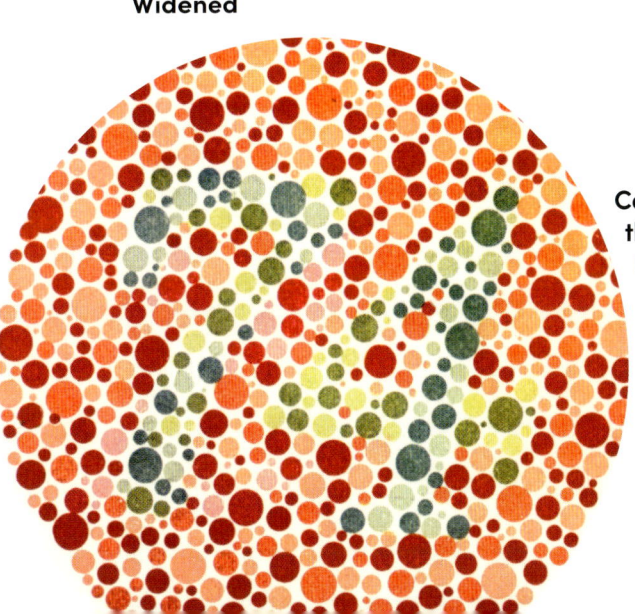

Can you see this number? If not, the pigment that picks up red light may be missing from your retina.

35

Smelly stuff

Humans have the ability to tell the difference between about a trillion smells! This incredible sense helps you to taste and enjoy things.

Up inside the nose, the cells have hairlike parts called cilia.

Sniff something?
Things have a smell because they give off particles called molecules. When you sniff something, these molecules travel up your nose, where there is a slimy substance called mucus (or snot).

Receiving smells

The molecules dissolve in the mucus. Then they move to special cells lining the top of your nose—here they are captured by smell receptors on the hairlike cilia.

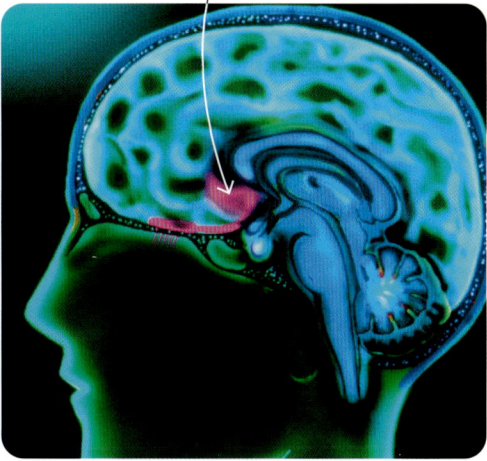

Smell receptor

A smell is recognized in an area toward the front of the brain.

A path to the brain

The smell receptors send a message to your brain, which either recognizes the smell or remembers it if it hasn't come across that smell before.

Fast facts

Mucus is a clear fluid. It mixes with things in the air and they give it a color.

Cells at the top of your nose produce about 2 pints (1 l) of mucus a day.

A bloodhound's sense of smell is 1,000 times better than a human's.

Super sneeze

If you have an allergic reaction to pollen, too much mucus will pour into your nose to try and flush it out. This makes you sneeze.

Fun with taste

Have you ever wondered what your tongue does? It helps you talk, but it also helps you move food around your mouth and, more importantly, taste it.

Fast facts

Your tongue has touch sensors, to help you feel food.

Special taste bud cells line the surface of your tongue. They help you taste food.

Glands inside your mouth produce a liquid called saliva.

Have a sniff
Smell plays an important part when you taste a food. That's why things don't taste so good if you have a blocked nose.

Salmon

Cocoa beans and chocolate

Ten thousand taste buds help you to tell the difference

Cherry

Cheese

If your frenulum is short, you will not be able to stick your tongue out very far.

Anchored in place
A flap of skin called the frenulum holds the bottom of your tongue to the floor of your mouth. It stops you from swallowing your tongue.

Saliva makes food easier to swallow, and also helps the taste buds detect the food's flavor.

Strawberry

Lemons

Mango

between five different flavors.

Tuna

Smaller papillae help the tongue to "grip" slippery food such as ice cream.

Larger, flat-topped papillae contain taste buds.

Fun flavors
When you chew food, pieces of it dissolve in saliva before you can sense its flavors. The taste bud cells on the tongue can detect five tastes: sweet, sour, bitter, salty, and umami (a savory taste in foods such as cheese).

Why the bumps?
Your tongue is bumpy so things don't slip off easily. It is covered in round papillae, some of which contain taste buds.

Take a bite

Teeth are very important for biting and chewing on food, which makes it easier to swallow. The "baby teeth" you have as a child will get replaced by adult teeth as you grow older.

Toothy set

We have different kinds of teeth for different functions. The front teeth (incisors) help bite food into smaller pieces. The large teeth at the back (molars) help grind down food. Inside each tooth are nerves and blood vessels.

Teeth are rooted in your gums.

Canines are slightly pointed. They help to tear food.

Incisors

An adult has 32 teeth, while a child has 20 baby teeth.

Why do they fall out?
Your baby teeth are small, and they don't grow in size to match your jaw as you become bigger. So they are pushed out between the ages of 6 and 12 to make room for larger, adult teeth.

X-ray shows an adult tooth waiting to push out the baby tooth above it.

Braces put a gentle pressure on each tooth.

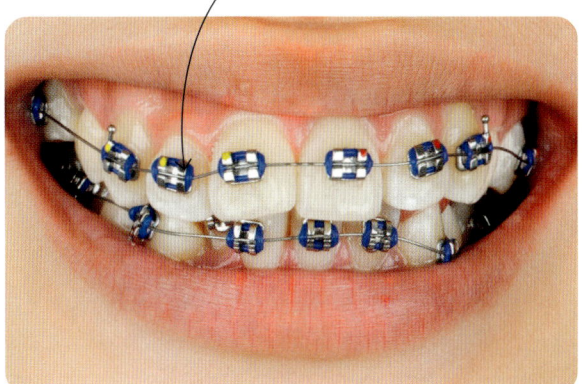

Why do I need braces?
Sometimes your teeth grow crookedly. Braces help straighten them, making them sit evenly in your mouth.

Keep on brushing
Pieces of food and saliva soon begin to coat your teeth with plaque, which can cause decay and lead to cavities. Daily brushing is important to remove plaque.

Digesting food

Food gives you the energy to live your life. When you eat food, it is broken down (digested) to release substances called nutrients, which help your body function properly as you grow.

Down the tube
After you have chewed your food, it is pushed down a tube called the esophagus and into your stomach.

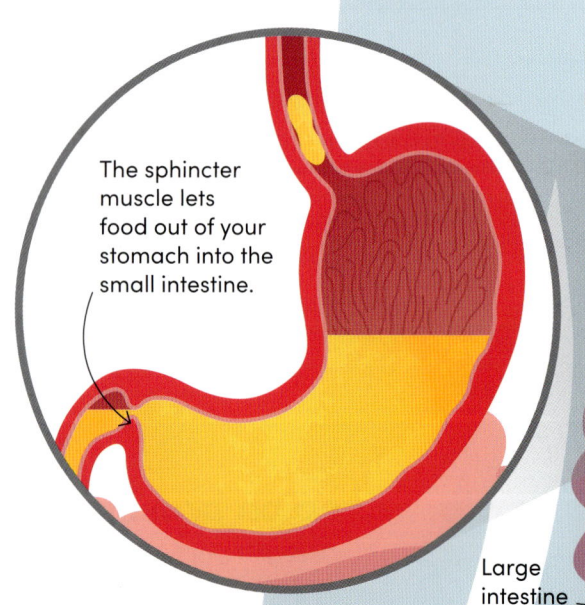

The sphincter muscle lets food out of your stomach into the small intestine.

Stomach

Liver

Large intestine

Small intestine

Acid bath
Acid is released in your stomach to break down the food. A constant churning helps turn the food into a mushy soup.

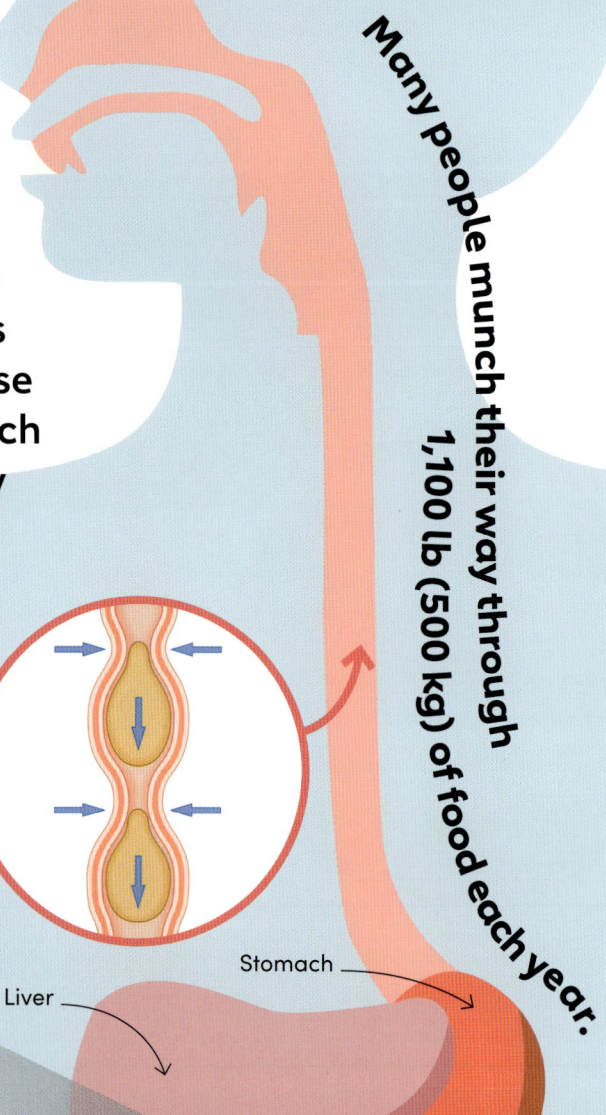

Many people munch their way through 1,100 lb (500 kg) of food each year.

42

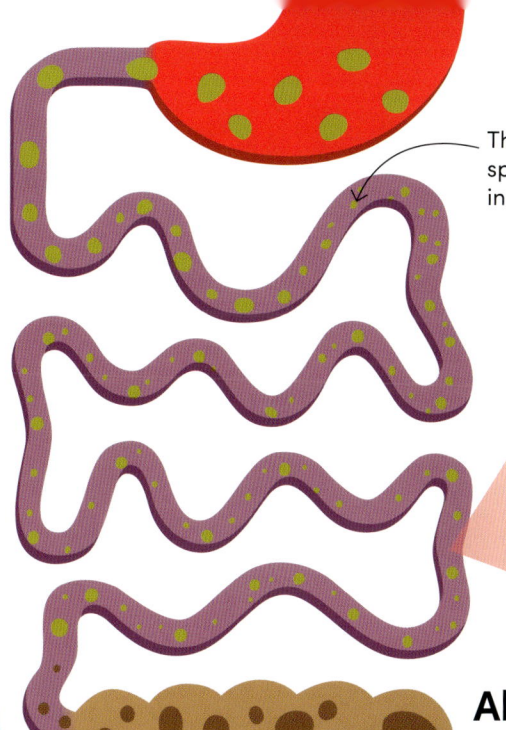

The broken-down food spends up to three hours in the small intestine.

Taking the nutrients
The small intestine is lined with fingerlike villi. Blood runs through these where it can pick up nutrients from the food and take them to the liver. The liver keeps what your body needs.

Half of the poop is made up of bacteria.

Absorbing water!
The remains of your food spend up to two days in the large intestine, which absorbs water from it. Strong muscles push it along.

Waiting to go
The rectum is where your poop is stored, waiting for you to go to the bathroom. This is waste that your body can't use.

Fast facts

Acid in your stomach could dissolve an iron nail.

A thick layer of mucus protects the stomach from its own acid.

Your small intestine is up to 23 ft (7 m) long.

👁 WATER TO PEE

Your body needs water to survive. So where does all the water you drink go? Water moves from the intestines to the blood. Your kidneys filter your blood to take out excess water and send it to the bladder where it is stored until you can pee.

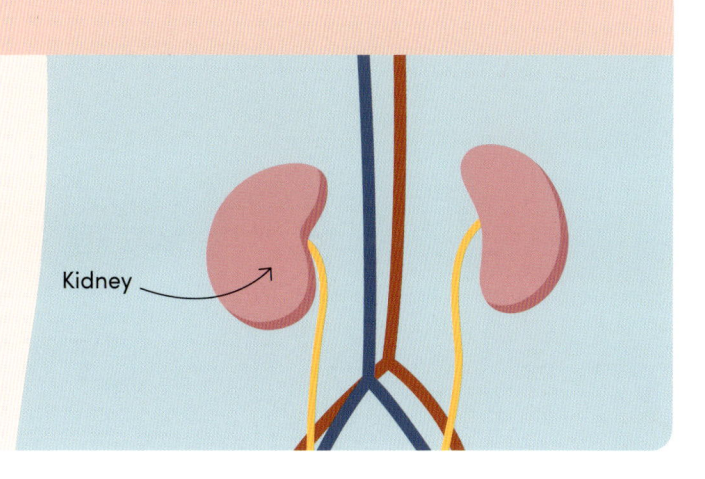

Kidney

Sleep tight

After all the activities you do each day, your body needs to rest. Sleep gives your brain a chance to catch up with what you've done. Without it, you cannot think properly and your body will begin to slow down.

Yawn away
If you are bored or sleepy, your breathing slows. You yawn to pull more oxygen into your body, helping to keep you awake.

Why do I dream?
Dreams bring pictures of things you have seen during the day, but also images that are unrelated to the day's events. Nobody knows exactly why people dream.

AWAKE OR ASLEEP?

Sometimes people walk in their sleep. They may even get dressed, or try to find something to eat. But when they wake up in the morning, they won't remember anything about it. Nobody really knows why people sleepwalk, but it is usually harmless. As children get older, most of them grow out of this behavior.

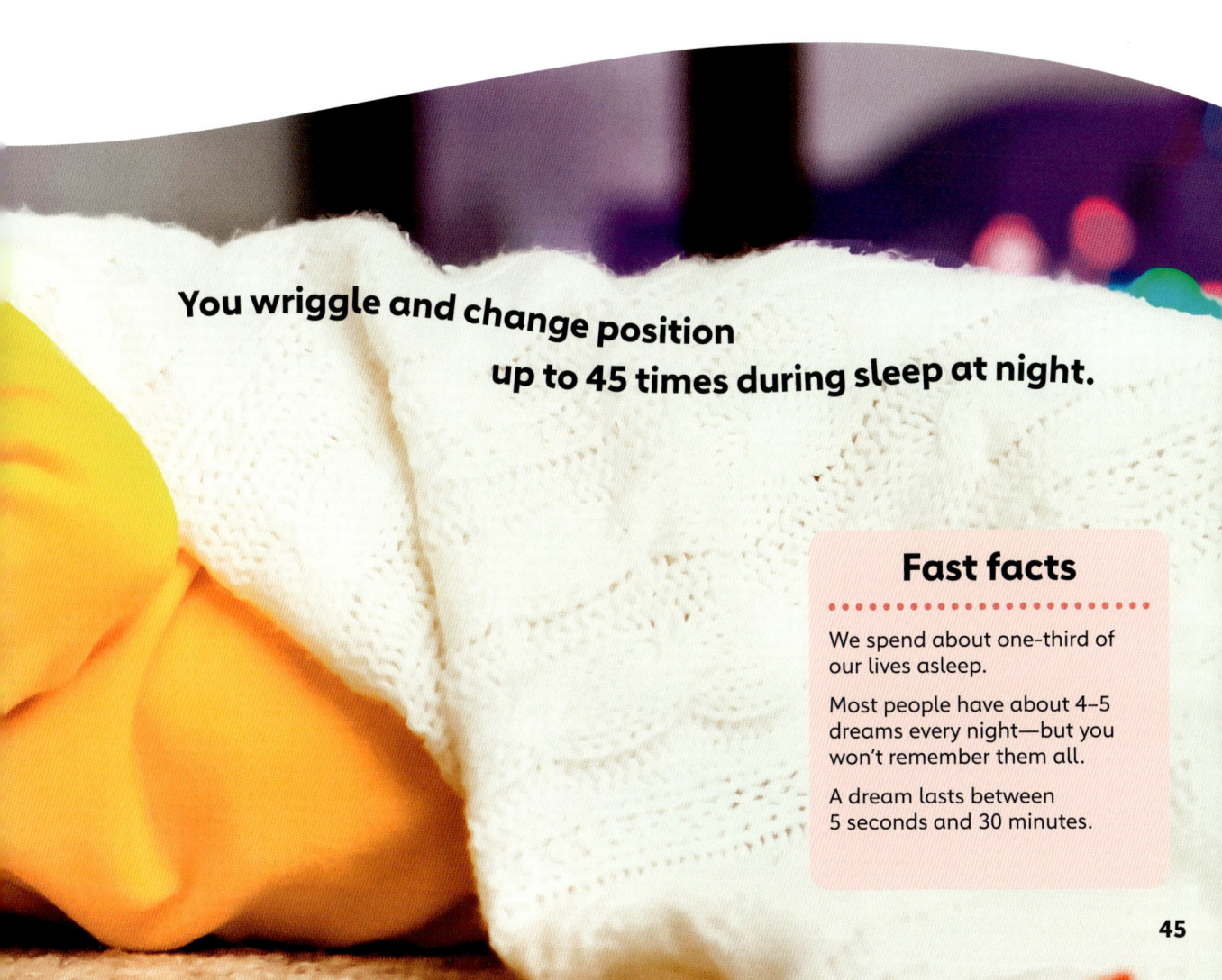

Nightmare alley
People sometimes have scary dreams called nightmares. Remember, nightmares are not real.

You wriggle and change position up to 45 times during sleep at night.

Fast facts

We spend about one-third of our lives asleep.

Most people have about 4–5 dreams every night—but you won't remember them all.

A dream lasts between 5 seconds and 30 minutes.

Facts match

What parts of the body are these clues describing? The answers can all be found in the pictures below.

1
This is made up of the **same stuff as your nails**. When you snip it off with scissors, it doesn't hurt.

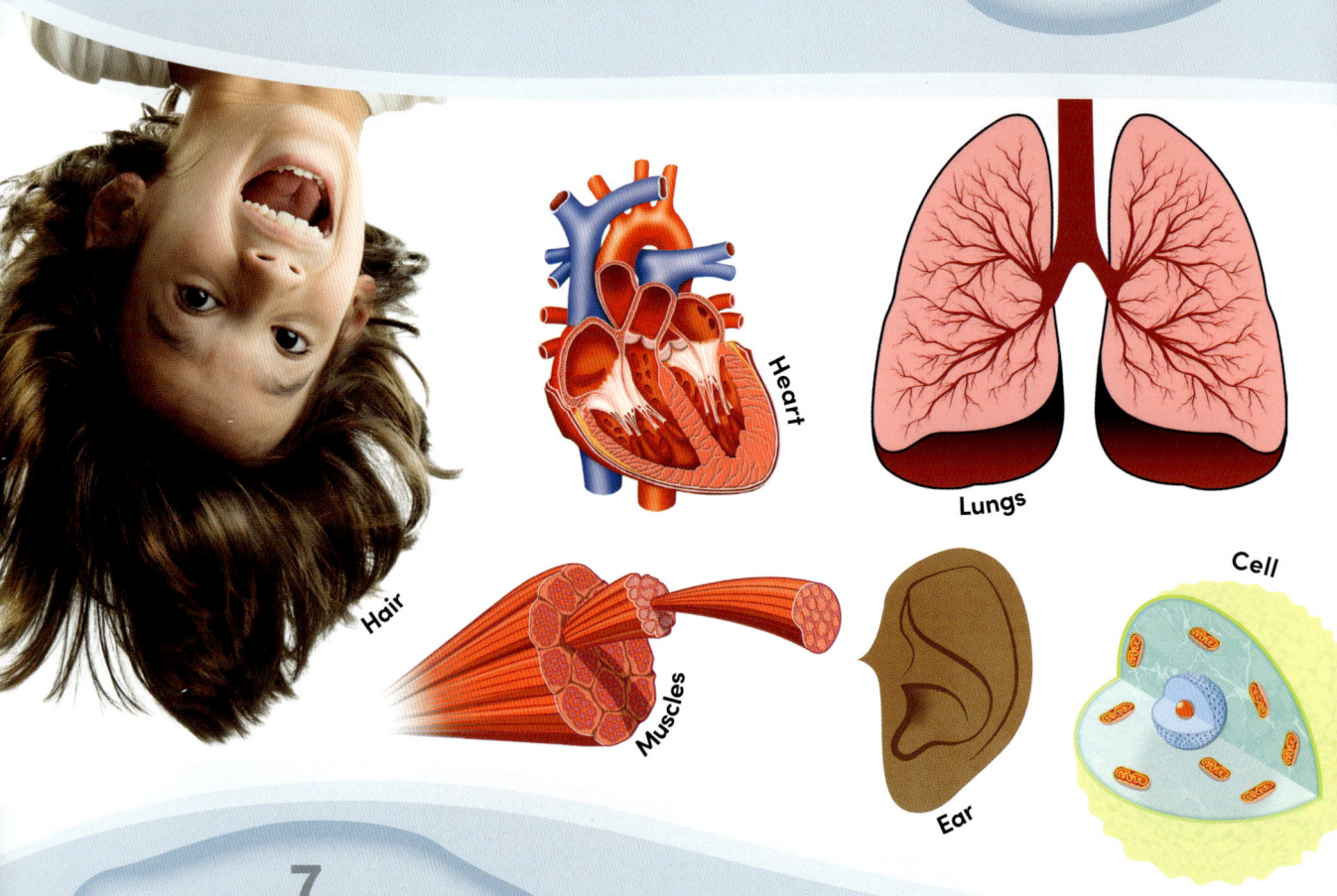

Hair

Heart

Lungs

Muscles

Ear

Cell

7
Wax in this body part **traps dust and dirt**, stopping it from entering your body.

8
This thigh bone is strong but light, with insides that look like **a spongy honeycomb**.

9
There are about **30 trillion** of these in your body. They have a control center called the nucleus.

10
These microbes **can multiply** only when inside your body.

2
Your body has two of these, and together they contain almost 1,500 miles (2,400 km) of air tubes.

3
These are your body's messengers, carrying signals from your skin to your brain.

5
This organ pushes blood around the body.

4
This organ is **like a computer for your body** and nearly everything you do is controlled by it.

6
This carries red blood cells, white blood cells, and platelets to different parts of the body.

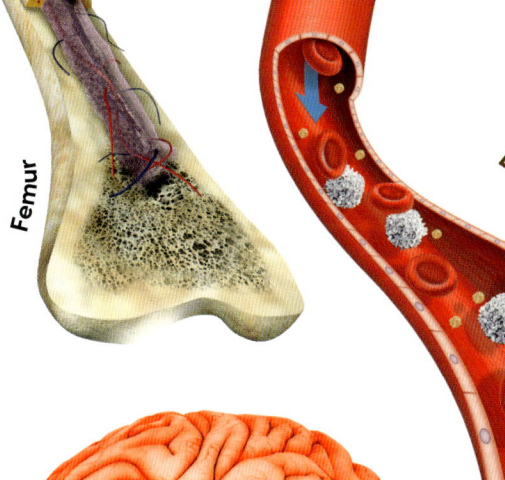

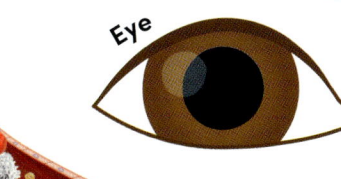

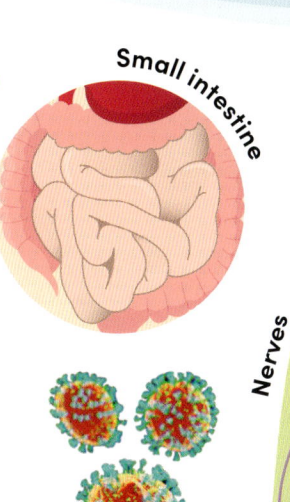

Femur

Eye

Small intestine

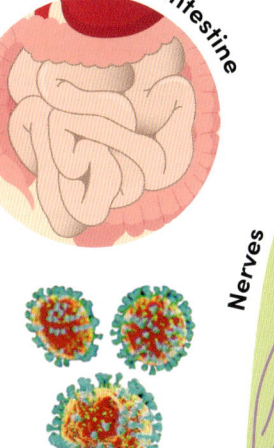

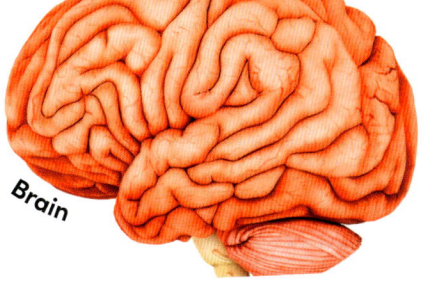

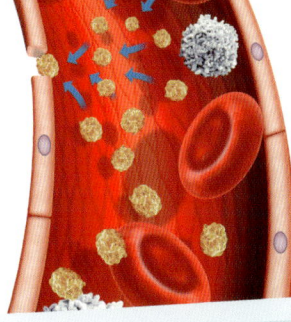

Artery

Nerves

Brain

Viruses

11
This is like **a tiny video camera** filled with fluid. It is directly connected to the brain.

12
Broken-down food stays in this organ in the digestive system for up to three hours.

13
These bundles are made of **tiny fibers**, and each fiber is thinner than a hair.

Answers: 1.Hair 2.Lungs 3.Nerves 4.Brain 5.Heart 6.Artery 7.Ear 8.Femur 9.Cell 10.Viruses 11.Eye 12.Small intestine 13.Muscles

Think away!

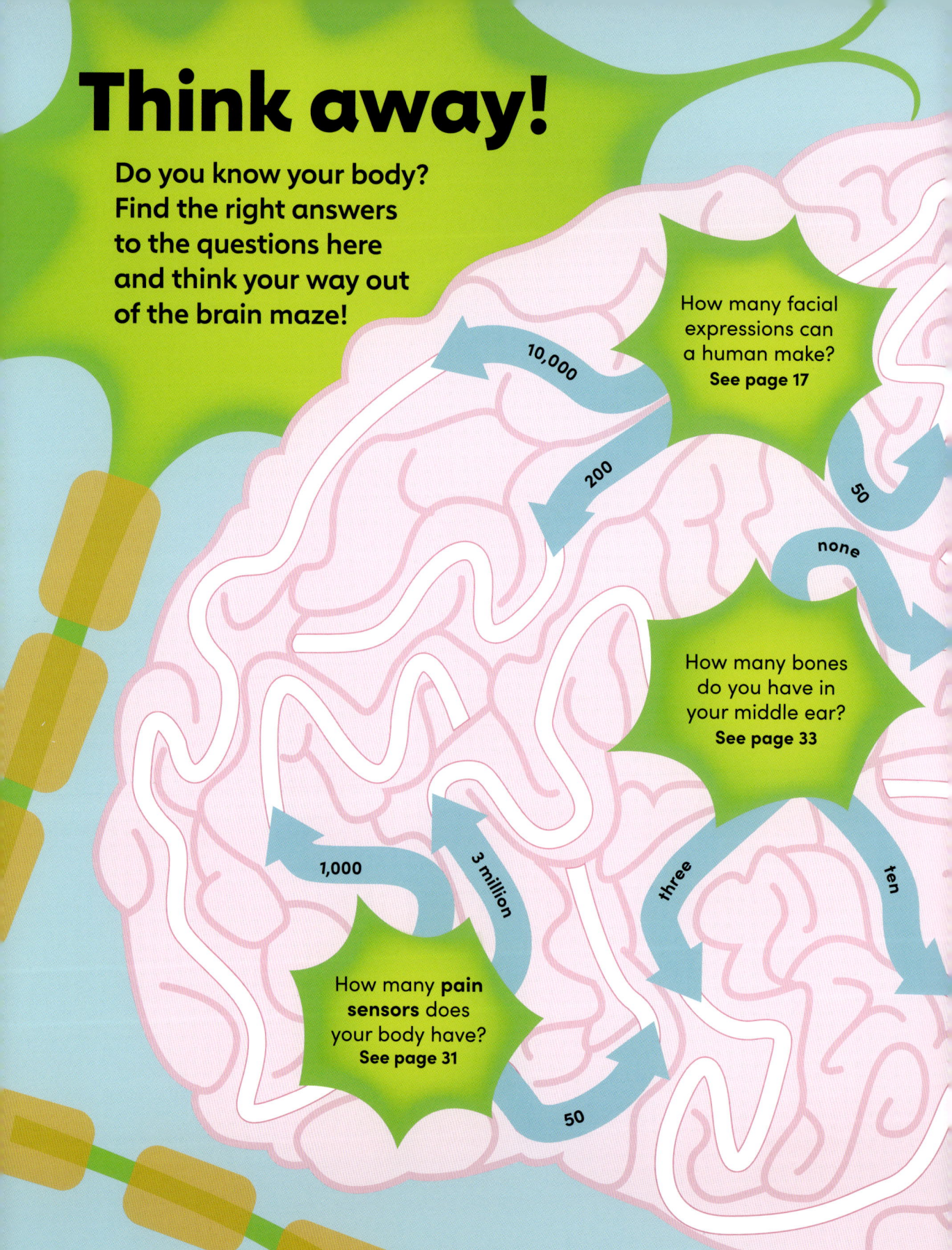

Do you know your body? Find the right answers to the questions here and think your way out of the brain maze!

How many facial expressions can a human make?
See page 17

How many bones do you have in your middle ear?
See page 33

How many pain sensors does your body have?
See page 31

10,000
200
50
none
1,000
3 million
three
ten
50

START HERE

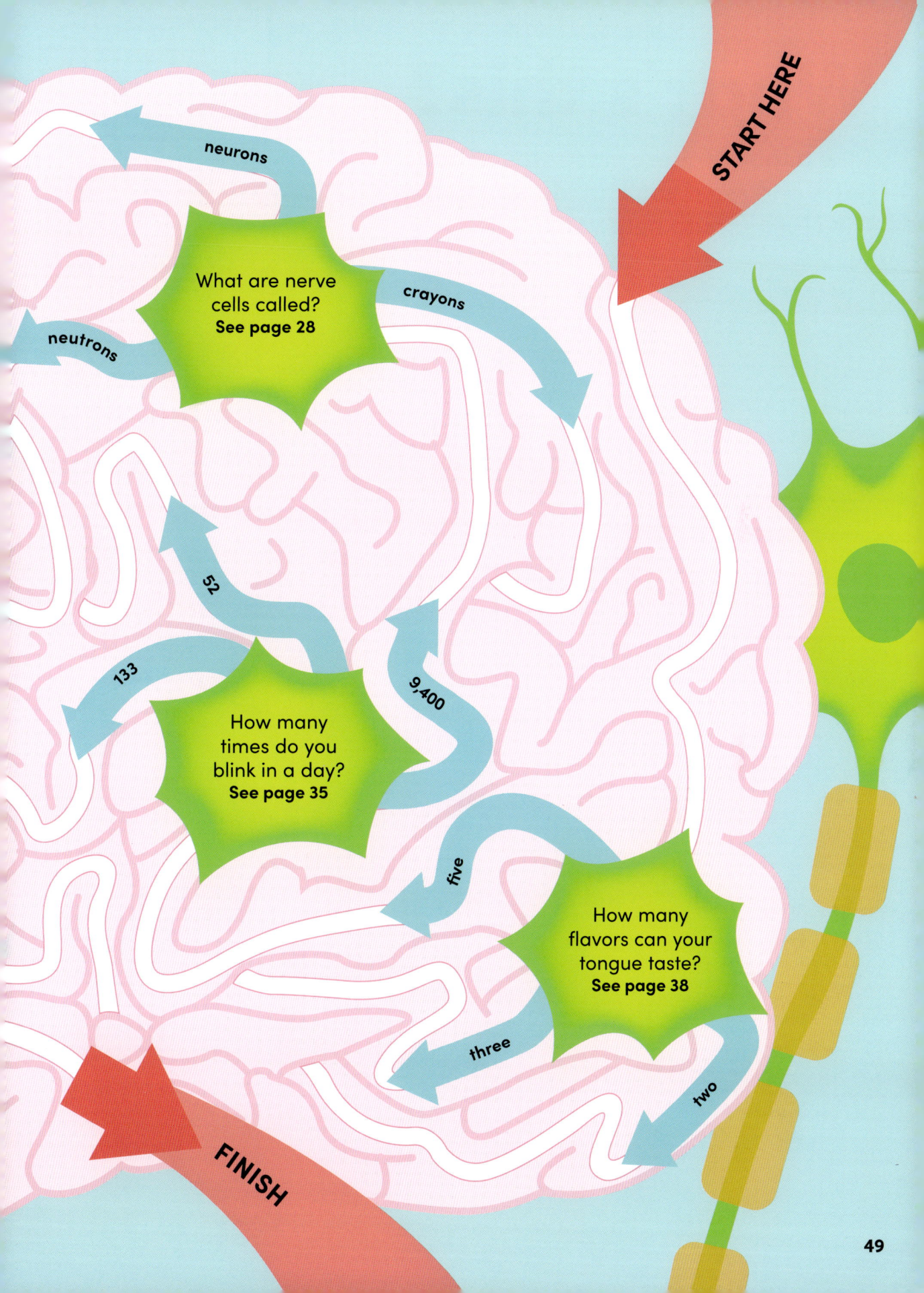

What are nerve cells called?
See page 28

neurons

neutrons

crayons

How many times do you blink in a day?
See page 35

52

133

9,400

How many flavors can your tongue taste?
See page 38

five

three

two

FINISH

What's this?

Take a look at these close-ups of body parts and see if you can identify them. The clues should help you!

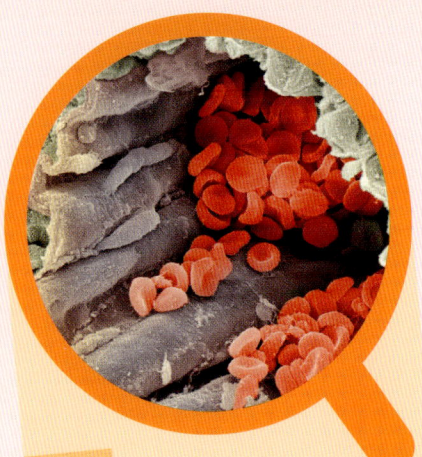

1
- This takes blood away from the heart.
- Its walls are thicker than a vein's walls.

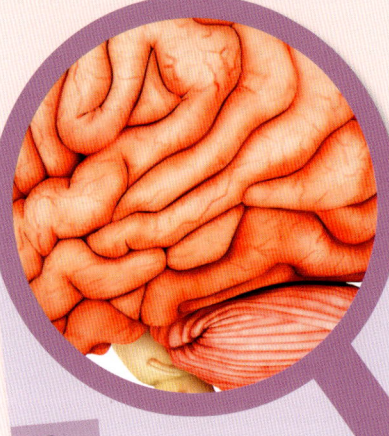

2
- As it grows, it wrinkles to fit your skull.
- It is split into two halves, called hemispheres.

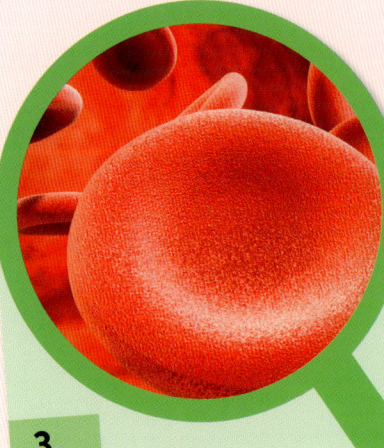

3
- They carry oxygen.
- They make up about 44 percent of your blood.

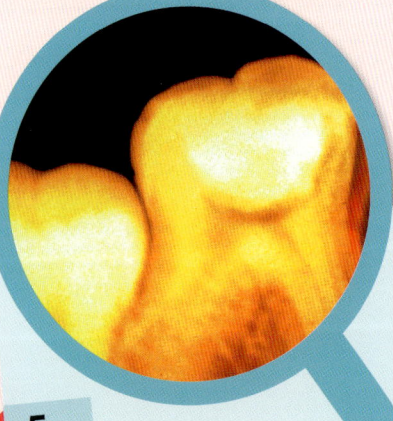

5
- They are rooted in your gums.
- The older ones are pushed out between the ages of 6 and 12 years.

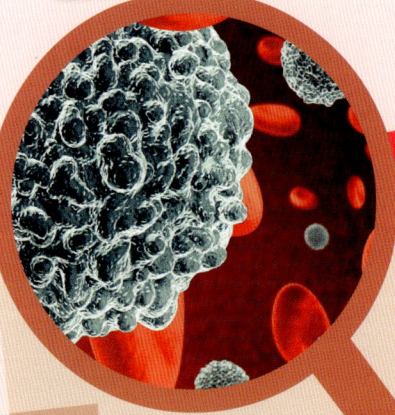

6
- They fight off germs in your body.
- Different types fight different germs.

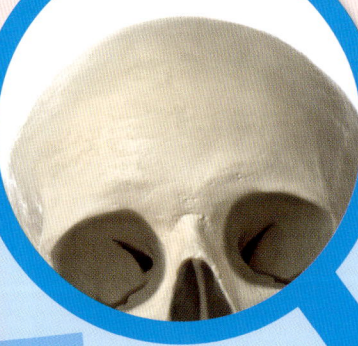

7
- Its top half is shaped like a dome.
- It houses the brain.

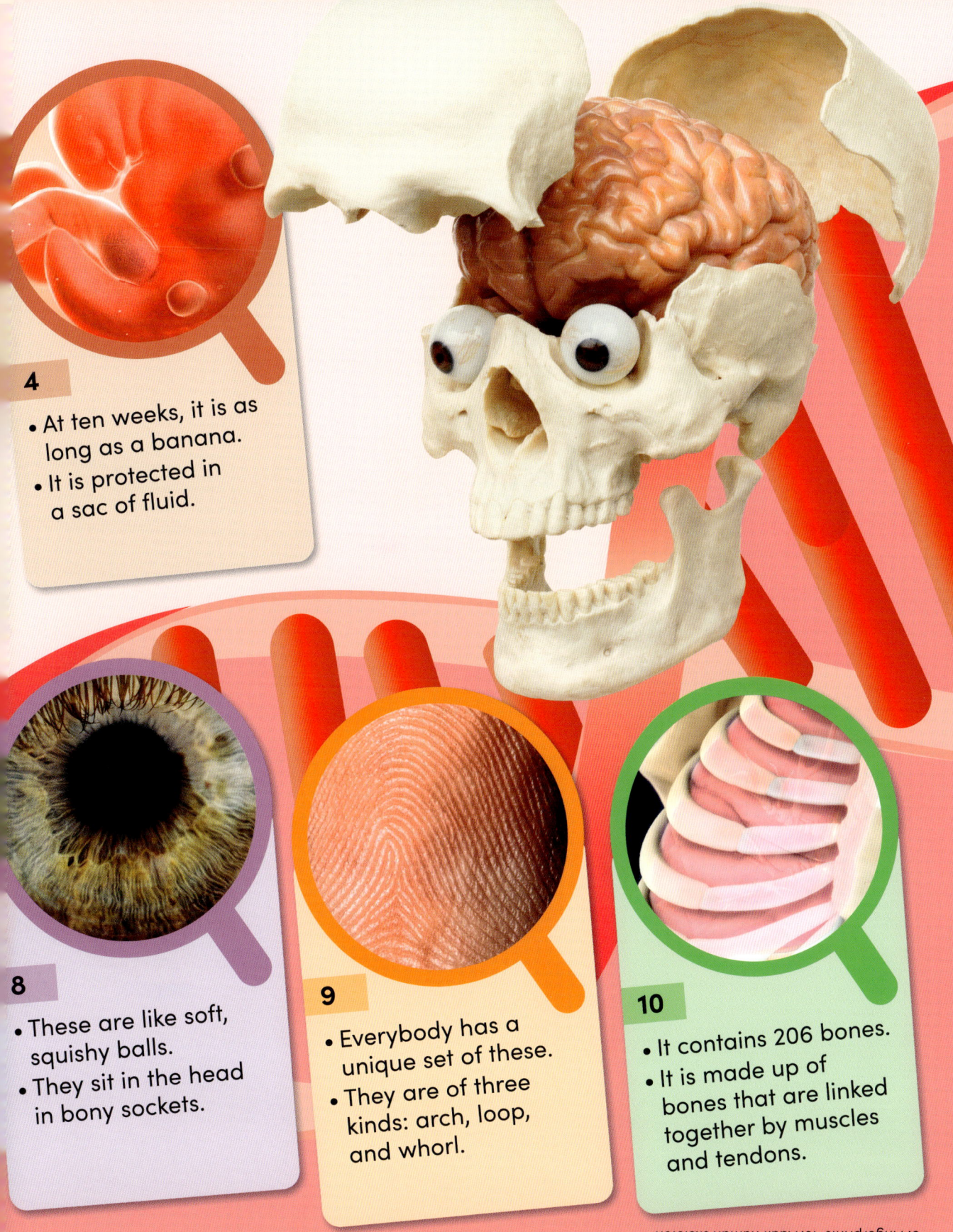

4
- At ten weeks, it is as long as a banana.
- It is protected in a sac of fluid.

8
- These are like soft, squishy balls.
- They sit in the head in bony sockets.

9
- Everybody has a unique set of these.
- They are of three kinds: arch, loop, and whorl.

10
- It contains 206 bones.
- It is made up of bones that are linked together by muscles and tendons.

Answers: 1. Artery 2. Brain 3. Red blood cells 4. A baby in a womb 5. Teeth 6. White blood cells 7. Skull 8. Eyes 9. Fingerprints 10. Adult human skeleton

Find the way!

You are a breath of fresh air! Can you travel to and from these lungs in a jiffy?

How to play

This is a game for up to four players.

You will need dice and a counter for each player. You could use counters from other board games you might have, or you could make your own counters with colored paper—one color for each player.

Each player takes turns to throw the dice, and begins from the START box. Follow the squares with each roll of the dice. If you land on an instruction, make sure you do as it says. Good luck!

The lungs don't work exactly like in this game. To find out more about the lungs, turn to pages 20–21.

Start

Finish

- You've just been inhaled. Move past the mucus in the nose quickly. **Move two spaces.**

- Did you get stuck in the mucus? You've been coughed out. **Move back to start!**

- You've reached the larynx. Jump on the vocal cords and make them dance for a second. **Miss a turn!**

- Back into the nose? No, try the mouth this time. Out you go. **Move two spaces.**

- Slide down the windpipe with glee. **Get another turn.**
- If you've rolled 4-5-6, take the long route. **Move right.**
- If you've rolled 1-2-3, take a short cut. **Move left.**
- Into the right lung you go. Slide right on from the tube on to the smaller tubes. **Move two spaces.**
- Enter the tiny alveoli and wait. **Miss a turn.**
- Are you late to meet your friend? Run fast. **Move one space.**
- Meet your buddy—blood—who has arrived from the heart! Give your oxygen to the blood and take their carbon dioxide. **Move one space.**
- You're caught in the chest. Wait to cough. **Move back one space.**
- Run back up the tubes and out of the lung. **Move three spaces.**
- Enter the left lung and sit here for a second. **Miss a turn.**

Glossary

Alveoli Tiny air sacs in the lungs where oxygen is passed into the blood.

Artery One of many vessels that carry blood from the heart to other parts of the body.

Blood vessel An artery, vein, or capillary that carries blood through the body.

Carbon dioxide A gas that humans breathe out.

Cartilage A tough, but bendy material that lines joints and makes up the structure of the nose and ears.

Cell The basic building block of the body.

Diaphragm A muscle across the chest just below the lungs, helping a person to breathe.

Digestion The process of breaking down food. This has two parts: the small intestine and the large intestine.

Esophagus A tube through which food moves from the throat to the stomach.

Germs Tiny bacteria and viruses that cause sickness.

Intestine A long tube through which food passes during the process of digestion.

Larynx A part of the throat where speech and other sounds are made.

Mucus A slippery fluid in areas such as the respiratory system.

Muscle A tissue that contracts to cause movement.

Nerve A bundle of neurons that carries information between the brain and body.

Nervous system A body system made of the brain, the spinal cord, and nerves that run between the spinal cord and the body.

Neuron A cell found in nerves.

Nutrients Substances in food that help the body function properly as it grows.

Organ One of a number of different parts of the body that each perform a particular job.

Oxygen A gas breathed in from the air. Humans need this gas to survive.

Papillae Tiny bumps on the surface of the tongue.

Plasma The clear liquid part of blood in which the blood cells move.

Poop The waste produced after digestion.

Reflex An automatic action. Often a reflex is triggered by the spinal cord or nerve clusters.

Saliva A liquid released into the mouth that helps dissolve food, and makes it slippery enough to swallow.

Senses The means by which humans find out about the world around them. The five main senses are hearing, sight, taste, touch, and smell.

Spinal cord A bundle of nerves that runs inside the backbone.

Sweat A liquid that is released onto the skin to help the body cool down.

Tendon A tough cord that links muscle to bone.

Trachea A tube that runs from the larynx to the lungs. Air moves through this "wind pipe" to and from the lungs.

Umbilical cord A cord that attaches a baby to the womb.

Vaccine A special medicine that teaches your body how to fight off infections.

Vein One of many vessels that carry blood from parts of the body to the heart.

Villi Fingerlike projections that line the wall of the small intestine through which nutrients are taken into the blood.

Voice box *see* larynx.

Womb The organ that houses a growing baby.

Index

AB
acid, stomach 25, 42, 43
allergies 25, 37
alveoli 30, 53
antibodies 25
arteries 19, 47, 50
babies 8–9, 27, 51
baby teeth 40, 41
bacteria 22, 23, 24, 43
biceps 16
bladder 43
blinking 35, 49
blood 18–19, 20, 43, 53
body language 27
body systems 6
bones 12–13, 51
braces 41
brain 28–29, 30, 31, 32, 33, 35, 37, 44, 47, 50
bronchi 53

CDE
carbon dioxide 20, 53
cardiovascular system 18–19
cartilage 12, 20
cells 7, 8, 9, 46
cilia 37
circulatory system 7, 18–19
clotting 11, 19
color blindness 35
communication 26–27
deafness 27, 32
diaphragm 21
digestive system 42–43
disease 22
dizziness 33
dreams 44, 45
ears 25, 32–33, 46, 48
eggs 8
endorphins 31
esophagus 42
exercise 17, 21
eyes 25, 29, 34–35, 47, 51

FGH
facial expressions 17, 26, 27, 48
femur 13, 47
fingerprints 11, 51
fingers 28, 29
flavors 39, 49
follicles 10, 14
food 38–39, 40, 41, 42–43
fractures 13
frenulum 38
germs 22–23, 24–25
gums 40, 50
hair 5, 14–15, 46
head lice 15
hearing 32–33
heart 7, 18, 46, 53
hemispheres 28, 50
hiccups 21
Hippocrates 22

IJKL
immune system 24–25
incisors 40
iron 5
joints 13
keratin 5, 14
kidneys 43
larynx 27, 52
lungs 20–21, 52–53

MNO
macrophages 24
microbes 22–23
molars 40
motor neurons 31
mouth 25, 38, 52
movement 16–17
mucus 25, 36, 43, 52
muscles 16–17, 29, 31, 46
nails 15
nerves 28, 47
neurons 28, 29, 31, 49
nightmares 45
nose 25, 29, 36, 37, 38, 52
nutrients 17, 42, 43
organs 6–7
oxygen 9, 19, 20–21, 53

PRS
pain 48
papillae 39
pee 43
plaque 41
plasma 19
platelets 19
poop 43
protein 17
pupils 35
rectum 43
red blood cells 19, 50
reflexes 31
retinas 35
saliva 25, 38, 39, 41
senses 29, 30–39
sensory neurons 31
sight 29, 34–35
sign language 27
skeleton 12–13, 51
skin 10–11, 30
sleep 44–45
sleepwalking 45
small intestine 42, 43, 47
smell 29, 36–37, 38
sneezing 25, 37
speech 27, 28
spinal cord 28
stomach 42
sweat 11

TUV
talking 26–27
taste 29, 36, 38–39
teeth 27, 40–41, 50
tendons 17
tissue 7
tongue 27, 29, 38–39
touch 29, 30–31
trachea (windpipe) 20, 53
triceps 16
twins 5
umbilical cord 9
vaccinations 23
viruses 22, 23, 47
vocal cords 52

WXY
water 21, 43
wax, ear 25, 32
white blood cells 23, 24, 25, 50
womb 8–9
X-rays 13
yawning 44

Acknowledgments

The publisher would like to thank the following people for their help with making the book: Lisa Jane Gillespie and the Inclusion & Impact Team for a sensitivity check, Samrajkumar S for picture credits, Carron Brown for proofreading, and Helen Peters for indexing.

The publisher would like to thank the following for their kind permission to reproduce their photographs:

(Key: a-above; b-below/bottom; c-center; f-far; l-left; r-right; t-top)

Adobe Stock: Anna 30–31tc, Engagestock 26br, Kai 38c, Petro 30bl, Scentrio 11tr, Shadowbird 38l; **Alamy Stock Photo:** BSIP SA / SGO 28bl, Darryl Fonseka 22–23bc, 47cb, Fotoshoot 45tr, Mauritius Images GmbH / Sebastian Frölich 38–39t, Robert Mora 35clb, Science History Images / Photo Researchers 13tl, 39cr, 51crb, Science Photo Library / CNRI 3tr, 23tr, Science Photo Library / Sciepro 8tr, 51tl, Science Photo Library / Steve Gschmeissner 10clb, 33cra, Christopher Stewart 25tc, Stocktrek Images, Inc. 29tr, 47clb, 50ca, SuperStock / Francisco Cruz / Purestock 33bl; **Depositphotos Inc:** DenysKuvaiev 36–37b, Djomas 26–27c, olenahs2.gmail.com 17br, Yanlev 30crb, Zurijeta 46cla; **Dorling Kindersley:** Arran Lewis / Zygote 13c; **Dreamstime.com:** Aoo3771 15cla, Yuri Arcurs 26tl, Art4stock 14bc, Ilshat Bikmiev 40–41bc, Blue Ring Education Pte Ltd 7ca, Yap Kee Chan 39clb, Pattarawit Chompipat 11tl, Melek Cimen 22clb, Jose Manuel Gelpi Diaz 3br, 14–15bc, Aleksey Eremeev 11ca, 51cb, Eveleen007 25cra, Liubomyr Feshchyn 27c, Guniita 35cra, Svetlana Iakusheva 51clb, Igorr 39cla, Kittipong Jirasukhanont 19cra, 50tr, Sebastian Kaulitzki 13cr, Kkovaleva 38cr, Kts 25cl, Anna Kucherova 38crb, Denys Kuvaiev 54–55, Kwanchaichaiudom 44tl, Nemes Laszlo 23cra, Maryna Melnyk 46cra, Volodymyr Melnyk 34 (Eyes), 34cla, Yoshiro Mizuta 15tc, Nataliia Mysak 17tc, Thorsten Nilson 50crb, Parinyabinsuk 37br, Prostockstudio 15crb, 44–45b, Alexander Raths 38cra, Serhiy Shullye 39cl, Skypixel 50cb, Valentyn75 39c, Tom Wang 26bl, Wavebreakmedia Ltd 34clb; **Getty Images:** DigitalVision / Catherine Delahaye 21cla, E+ / FG Trade 32bl, Moment / Catherine Falls Commercial 45tl, Moment / Oscar Wong 8–9b, Moment / Svetlana Repnitskaya 41tl, Photodisc / Jonathan Knowles 35cb, Science Photo Library / Sciepro 18c, Stone / Flashpop 14l; **Getty Images / iStock:** Baytunc 11crb, ChenRobert 21tr, DDurrich 25br, E+ / FG Trade 26tr, E+ / JGalione 27cra, E+ / Kali9 4–5b, E+ / Portishead1 28–29b, E+ / Riska 40, EyeEm Mobile GmbH 5tr, Arianne de San Jose van Hoof 30cla, InnaVlasova 27tl, Insta_Photos 27br, Anthony Lee 34, MangoStar_Studio 10–11c, Andriy Nekrasov 31bc, Photo_Concepts 23crb, Princessdlaf 21br; **Photolibrary:** Steve Allen 35bc; **Science Photo Library:** A. Dowsett, National Infection 22–23tc, 1, 12, 24, Biophoto Associates 13bc, BSIP VEM 37cra, 41cla, 50clb, Gregory Dimijian 35tl, Steve Gschmeissner 19cl, 31clb, 36cra, 37bl, 50cla, Dr Kari Lounatmaa 22tl, Lennart Nilsson, TT 8cl, D. Phillips 20bl, Philippe Plailly 18cb, Dr. Richard Kessel And Dr. Gene Shih 43tc; **Shutterstock.com:** Kksakultap 41cr, Teseo Ruiz 35clb (Normal).

Cover images: Front: **Dorling Kindersley:** Arran Lewis / Zygote c; **Dreamstime.com:** Blue Ring Education Pte Ltd bc, Pattarawit Chompipat cl, Darryl Fonseka cr, Jeremys78 cr/ (Tooth), Kittipong Jirasukhanont cla/ (Red Blood Cells), Kkovaleva cra/ (Cheese), Nemes Laszlo crb; **Getty Images:** Universal Images Group / BSIP bl; **Photolibrary:** Steve Allen crb/ (Color Blind); **Science Photo Library:** cra, CNRI cla, Steve Gschmeissner ca/ (Smell Receptors), Steve Gschmeissner ca, Dr Kari Lounatmaa cb; **Shutterstock.com:** Teseo Ruiz cb/ (Eye); Back: **Dreamstime.com:** Igorr ca, Yoshiro Mizuta cb, Valentyn75 clb; **Science Photo Library:** A. Dowsett, National Infection cr, Gregory Dimijian tl.